DEADLY DISEASES AND EPIDEMICS

MALARIA

Second Edition

DEADLY DISEASES AND EPIDEMICS

DEADLY DISEASES AND EPIDEMICS

MALARIA

Second Edition

Bernard Marcus, Ph.D.

CONSULTING EDITOR

Hilary Babcock, M.D., M.P.H.,
Infectious Diseases Division,
Washington University School of Medicine,
Medical Director of Occupational Health (Infectious Diseases),
Barnes-Jewish Hospital and St. Louis Children's Hospital

FOREWORD BY

David Heymann
World Health Organization

CHELSEA HOUSE
PUBLISHERS
An imprint of Infobase Publishing

In Memory of Ed Alcamo: Friend and Colleague

Deadly Diseases and Epidemics: Malaria, Second Edition

Chelsea House
An imprint of Infobase Publishing
132 West 31st Street
New York, NY 10001

Library of Congress Cataloging-in-Publication Data
Marcus, Bernard A.
    Malaria / Bernard A. Marcus ; consulting editor, Hilary Babcock ; foreword by David Heymann. — 2nd ed.
       p. cm. — (Deadly diseases and epidemics)
    Includes bibliographical references and index.
    ISBN-13: 978-1-60413-281-6 (hardcover : alk. paper)
    ISBN-10: 1-60413-281-7 (hardcover : alk. paper) 1. Malaria. 2. Malaria—History. I. Title. II. Series.

    RA644.M2M213 2009
    614.5'32—dc22
                                    2008045402

Table of Contents

Foreword

Communicable diseases kill and cause long-term disability. The microbial agents that cause them are dynamic, changeable, and resilient: they are responsible for more than 14 million deaths each year, mainly in developing countries.

Approximately 46 percent of all deaths in the developing world are due to communicable diseases, and almost 90 percent of these deaths are from AIDS, tuberculosis, malaria, and acute diarrheal and respiratory infections of children. In addition to causing great human suffering, these high-mortality communicable diseases have become major obstacles to economic development. They are a challenge to control either because of the lack of effective vaccines, or because the drugs that are used to treat them are becoming less effective because of antimicrobial drug resistance.

Millions of people, especially those who are poor and living in developing countries, are also at risk from disabling communicable diseases such as polio, leprosy, lymphatic filariasis, and onchocerciasis. In addition to human suffering and permanent disability, these communicable diseases create an economic burden—both on the work force that handicapped persons are unable to join, and on their families and society, upon which they must often depend for economic support.

Finally, the entire world is at risk of the unexpected communicable diseases, those that are called emerging or re-emerging infections. Infection is often unpredictable because risk factors for transmission are not understood, or because it often results from organisms that cross the species barrier from animals to humans. The cause is often viral, such as Ebola and Marburg hemorrhagic fevers and severe acute respiratory syndrome (SARS). In addition to causing human suffering and death, these infections place health workers at great risk and are costly to economies. Infections such as Bovine Spongiform Encephalopathy (BSE) and the associated new human variant of Creutzfeldt-Jakob Disease (vCJD) in Europe, and avian influenza A (H5N1) in Asia, are reminders of the seriousness of emerging and re-emerging infections. In addition, many of these infections have the potential to cause pandemics, which are a constant threat to our economies and public health security.

Science has given us vaccines and anti-infective drugs that have helped keep infectious diseases under control. Nothing demonstrates the effectiveness of vaccines better than the successful eradication of smallpox, the decrease in polio as the eradication program continues, and the decrease in measles when routine immunization programs are supplemented by mass vaccination campaigns.

Likewise, the effectiveness of anti-infective drugs is clearly demonstrated through prolonged life or better health in those infected with viral diseases such as AIDS, parasitic infections such as malaria, and bacterial infections such as tuberculosis and pneumococcal pneumonia.

But current research and development is not filling the pipeline for new anti-infective drugs as rapidly as resistance is developing, nor is vaccine development providing vaccines for some of the most common and lethal communicable diseases. At the same time, providing people with access to existing anti-infective drugs, vaccines, and goods such as condoms or bed nets—necessary for the control of communicable diseases in many developing countries—remains a great challenge.

Education, experimentation, and the discoveries that grow from them are the tools needed to combat high mortality infectious diseases, diseases that cause disability, or emerging and re-emerging infectious diseases. At the same time, partnerships between developing and industrialized countries can overcome many of the challenges of access to goods and technologies. This book may inspire its readers to set out on the path of drug and vaccine development, or on the path to discovering better public health technologies by applying our present understanding of the human genome and those of various infectious agents. Readers may likewise be inspired to help ensure wider access to those protective goods and technologies. Such inspiration, with pragmatic action, will keep us on the winning side of the struggle against communicable diseases.

David L. Heymann
Assistant Director General
Health Security and Environment
Representative of the Director General for Polio Eradication
World Health Organization
Geneva, Switzerland

1

On the Wings of Mosquitoes

In 1942, U.S. Navy Pharmacist's Mate First Class Louis Ortega accompanied the U.S. Marines to Guadalcanal. According to Ortega, "When you got malaria, you might have it five times. Everybody was getting it over and over again. I had it five times—twice on the island and three times in Australia. Those were reoccurrence attacks. If they evacuated people who had it five times there would have been no one left in the field. By the first of December, we had more casualties—4,000 or 5,000 casualties—from malaria [and] dengue fever, than we did from actual battle." Ortega went on to describe Marines being relocated to Brisbane, Australia, where they were "stuck in a swamp loaded with mosquitoes. So they were always in the hospital."[1]

BATTLE ZONE

In the autumn of 1942, American Marines were dug into the sands on the island of Guadalcanal in the South Pacific, about to face one of the bloodiest battles in World War II. The Japanese had occupied Guadalcanal and the surrounding islands since January of that year. In August, the Marines gained control of the island, but the Japanese did not retreat quietly. Fierce fighting continued through February 1943. However, in the autumn, while the Marines worried about the coming battle and the enemy they had to face, mosquitoes hummed about them incessantly and bit them mercilessly, especially after dark. The mosquitoes were at their worst just after dusk and just before dawn. Sleeping under those conditions was probably next to impossible. Perhaps the Marines did not worry about the mosquitoes as much as they did about the coming battle, but perhaps they should have. The mosquitoes were more than just a nuisance.

Thanks to the development of **antibiotics**, World War II was possibly the first war in history where more men died from wounds suffered in battle than from infections. Previously, those who were not mortally wounded often developed infections that could not be cured, and in the crowded, stressful, dirty conditions of battle, contagious infections passed easily from one person to another, especially if soldiers were malnourished. However, Guadalcanal and perhaps other rain forest-covered South Pacific islands remained places where illness took more lives than did fighting (Table 1.1).

Table 1.1   Diseases of Entomological Importance: World War II, United States Armed Forces, 1940–1945

Disease	1940–1941	1942–1943	1942–1945
Dengue fever	656	23,192	84,093
Diarrhea, Dysentery	20,976	199,505	523,331
Filariasis	0	–	1,653
Malaria	8,233	178,594	460,936
Sand fly fever	0	–	12,438
Scabies	–	21,286	–
Typhus	0	0	7,352

Source: Statistical Health Reports, Division of Medical Statistics, Office of the Surgeon General, Department of the Army.

Seventeen hundred American men died from wounds suffered during the Battle of Guadalcanal. Four to five thousand died of the disease spread by the mosquitoes: malaria. The Japanese may have suffered even higher casualties, from both the fighting and the mosquitoes. When wounded American survivors were evacuated to Australia, many were placed in a particular hospital near a swamp, where mosquitoes spread the disease among them even more. Indeed, at one point, General Douglas MacArthur, Commander of U.S. forces in the Southwest Pacific during World War II, is said to have complained that at any time, one-third of his troops had malaria and another third was recovering from it. In fact, it was not until commanders were made responsible for their troops' health

MOSQUITO TAXONOMY

Taxonomy is the branch of biology that deals with the classification of plants and animals. It begins with a broad, all-inclusive category, the kingdom. Each category is divided into more specific subcategories that are based on particular characteristics of the organisms being classified. The following is the taxonomy of the *Anopheles* genus, to which malaria-carrying mosquitoes belong.

KINGDOM: Animals

   PHYLUM: Arthropoda (animals with paired, jointed legs, and an external skeleton)

      CLASS: Insecta (arthropods with three pairs of jointed legs)

         ORDER: Diptera (flies—insects with one pair of wings)

            FAMILY: Culicidae (the mosquitoes)

               GENUS: *Anopheles*

that precautionary measures were taken to avoid malarial infection. Troops were ordered to take **quinine** tablets daily to avoid becoming infected. Once the administering of quinine tablets became policy, malaria was brought under control, and the Americans could go about their task of winning the war in the Pacific.

MOSQUITO-BORNE DISEASE

Malaria is one of many diseases spread by mosquitoes, and mosquitoes are by no means the only **arthropods** (small animals with jointed legs, including the mosquitoes) that feed on human blood and spread disease.

The blood of an animal is a rich source of nourishment for any other organism that can take advantage of it. Small animals, such as mosquitoes and other blood-sucking arthropods, are well adapted to such a lifestyle because they are usually able to make contact with their victims without being detected, grab a quick meal, and disappear without being swatted. Other much larger animals, like the sea lamprey of the Great Lakes and Atlantic Ocean, readily feed on the blood of large fish like salmon or lake trout. Organisms that feed on the tissues of animals without killing them first are referred to as **parasites**. Those that do so without actually entering the bodies of their victims are referred to as **ectoparasites**. Ectoparasites survive by feeding on other animals, but they do not kill them in the process. Mosquitos are ectoparasites. There are still other parasites—usually smaller organisms—that live inside their victims and, consequently, inside their nutrient supply. Such parasites do not have to go looking for a meal when they are hungry, nor do they worry much about being eaten by other animals. Such parasites are known as **endoparasites**. The organism that causes malaria (*Plasmodium*) is an endoparasite. A problem that theses parasites do face, however, is what to do should their host die. When that happens, the parasites within die as well, and it is not in a parasite's best interest to kill its host. Some endoparasites get around this problem by hitching a ride from one victim to another via an ectoparasite. Such is the case with malaria, which is transported from victim to victim within a mosquito.

Human malaria is always transmitted by a mosquito of the genus *Anopheles*. There are over 400 species of *Anopheles* mosquitoes, of which perhaps 60 can carry malaria. Mosquitoes of other genera may carry malaria among other animals, such as birds, but they appear to be incapable of spreading the disease among humans, even if they bite someone who is infected with the parasite. Moreover, malaria that affects other animals cannot be transferred to people. A specific relationship appears to exist among each type of malaria, each species of animal it affects, and the mosquito species that carries it. Only human malaria affects people, and only some specific species of *Anopheles* mosquitoes are capable of transmitting it.

Generally, an endoparasite such as the organism that causes malaria is referred to by biologists as simply a parasite. The mosquito that spreads it is called a **vector**. The victim within

SOME MOSQUITO-BORNE DISEASES

dengue fever

eastern equine encephalitis

elephantiasis

Japanese encephalitis

LaCrosse encephalitis

malaria

western equine encephalitis

West Nile virus

yellow fever

SOME BLOOD-SUCKING ARTHROPODS AND THE DISEASES THEY SPREAD

black flies: river blindness

fleas: bubonic plague

reduviid bugs: Chagas disease

sandflies: leishmaniasis (kala-azar)

ticks: Lyme disease, Rocky Mountain spotted fever, typhus

tsetse flies: sleeping sickness

whom the parasite lives is called the **host**. Although malaria may have been brought under control among American servicemen in the South Pacific in World War II, it affects millions of people worldwide today. As of 2004, 3.2 billion people lived in Malaria-prone areas.[2] Each year there are approximately 100 million new cases of malaria and 1 million deaths associated with it, 850,000 of which are children.

Malaria is a complex disease that may occur in four different forms. The disease is caused by a **protozoan** of the genus *Plasmodium*, and it is spread by mosquitoes of the genus *Anopheles*. It has caused illness, suffering, and death, and it has had a major impact on human history. Today, malaria remains a serious medical challenge in much of the world, particularly in Africa.

This book describes the *Plasmodium* life cycle, the *Anopheles* life cycle as well as the origin and ecology of the disease, and the impact of malaria on history. The book also discusses the medical diagnosis and treatment of malaria, as well as its control and prevention. The book concludes with an examination of the current state of malaria and what the future may hold.

2

A Complex Life Cycle

One means of controlling malaria is by disturbing the life cycle of the mosquito vector, and one way of doing that is by depriving it of a place for its larvae to develop. Between 1976 and 1983, an experiment carried out in the San Francisco Bay tested draining tidal pools by ditches. Pools filled normally at high tide, but the drainage ditches allowed the pools to empty when the tide receded. Consequently, mosquito larvae no longer had protected nurseries in which to develop. Instead, they had to follow the draining water through the ditches and into the open water, where they were vulnerable to predation. The result was a reduction in mosquitoes without serious ecological damage to the bay and its biodiversity.[1]

The term "malaria" originates from the Italian word *mal'aria*, meaning "bad air." The Romans knew about malaria 2,000 years ago. They believed that malaria was caused by foul air that resulted from fermentation that seeped out of marshes and swamps. It is now known that malaria is spread by *Anopheles* mosquitoes. The disease is caused by a protozoan, a single-celled endoparasite of the genus *Plasmodium*.

THE PARASITE

There are more than 50 species of *Plasmodium*, only four of which cause human malaria: *Plasmodium falciparum*, *Plasmodium malariae*, *Plasmodium ovale*, and *Plasmodium vivax*. *Plasmodium vivax* is the most common. It usually causes a mild and very rarely fatal form of malaria. Similarly, *Plasmodium ovale* causes a mild infection. *Plasmodium malariae* causes a severe fever, but it is not usually life threatening. In contrast, *Plasmodium falciparum* causes severe infection that kills millions of people every year worldwide. *Plasmodium falciparum* is the organism that causes the form of malaria that is typically thought of whenever the disease is mentioned. *Plasmodium malariae* is often referred to as "quartan" malaria, meaning the fever and other symptoms run in four-day cycles. Other forms of malaria are "tertian," meaning that the symptoms occur in three-day cycles.

The *Plasmodium* life cycle (Figure 2.1) is described as an **alternation of generations**. This means an asexually reproducing generation, which reproduces by splitting in two, alternates with a generation that reproduces by forming sex cells that fuse with one another and produce individuals with new combinations of traits.

When an infected mosquito bites a person, the *Plasmodium* parasites enter the blood and head immediately for the liver. Within 30 minutes to one hour, all of the parasites have penetrated the liver; none remain in the circulating blood. Once inside the liver, the organisms multiply asexually, which means that each one divides into two identical copies of itself. They continue this reproduction in the liver cells for 9 to 16 days, after which they emerge from the liver and invade red blood cells. The parasites mature in the red blood cells, where they feed on hemoglobin and continue to reproduce asexually.

PLASMODIUM TAXONOMY

KINGDOM: Protista

PHYLUM: Apicomplexa

CLASS: Sporozoasida

ORDER: Eucoccidiorida

FAMILY: Plasmodiidae

GENUS: *Plasmodium*

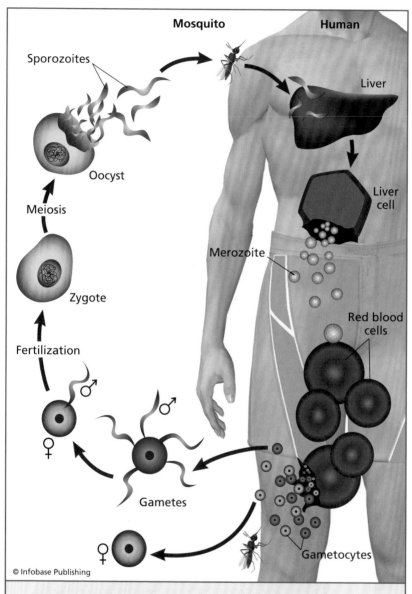

Mosquito　　　　　Human

Sporozoites

Oocyst

Liver

Liver cell

Meiosis

Merozoite

Zygote

Red blood cells

Fertilization

Gametes

Gametocytes

© Infobase Publishing

Figure 2.1 This diagram shows the complex life cycle of *Plasmodium* and how mosquitoes operate as a vector that transmits this parasite to humans, causing them to become sick with malaria.

Eventually they burst out of the blood cells, rupturing them in the process.

After the first few reproductive cycles in the red blood cells, the maturation of all of the parasites becomes more or less coordinated, and the blood cells begin to rupture quite simultaneously. As the blood cells burst, the parasites and their waste products are released. The newly liberated parasites quickly infect new cells. This series of events repeats several times. Eventually, however, the asexual stage of the malaria cycle comes to an end, and the final generation of parasites emerges from the blood cells. Most of them reinvade the liver, where they may remain for a long time.

Some of these newly emerged parasites, however, become sexually reproducing cells. If an *Anopheles* mosquito bites a person when these cells are present in the blood and picks up any of them, the malarial life cycle continues into its sexually reproducing generation.

If a mosquito of a genus other than *Anopheles* bites someone with malaria, it simply digests any malarial cells that it swallows. However, *Plasmodium* can resist the digestive chemicals of the *Anopheles* mosquito digestive system, and when an *Anopheles* mosquito swallows the malarial reproductive cells that it has obtained from an infected victim's blood, each of the cells fuses with another in the mosquito's gut. The cells that result are described as **diploid**, because they have two sets of structurally identical chromosomes: one from each of the cells that produced them. These new cells penetrate the wall of the mosquito's intestine. In the intestine, they undergo **meiosis**, a form of cell division that returns their chromosome number to one set per cell, known as **haploid**. These cells continue to divide, but they do not remain in the intestinal wall. Instead, after about ten days to two weeks, they migrate to the mosquito's salivary gland. When the mosquito bites a subsequent victim, it injects the parasites into the victim. The mosquito remains capable of infecting every person it bites until it dies. Infection with malaria parasites seems to make mosquitoes more active feeders.

Each of the four types of malaria has its own life cycle. *Plasmodium falciparum* has a faster reproductive rate and a shorter incubation period before symptoms of malaria show than do the other species. For example, it takes *Plasmodium malariae* up to 72 hours to complete a single generation inside a human host's red blood cells. *Plasmodium vivax* does it in 43 hours. *Plasmodium falciparum* takes as little as 36 hours to complete a generation in a human host's red blood cells. Additionally, *Plasmodium falciparum* may occupy as many as 60 percent of its host's red blood cells. Other malaria species usually occupy fewer than 2 percent.

AN INTRODUCTION TO PARASITOLOGY

Some parasites, such as *Plasmodium*, are incapable of surviving outside of a host organism. Thus, if this parasite kills its host, it guarantees its own death unless a compatible transporting agent, such as a mosquito, picks it up. For this reason, a successful parasite is usually most at home in an organism that has a tolerance for that parasite. The parasite can complete its life cycle in such an organism without killing the organism or even making it sick. For example, the parasite that causes African sleeping sickness routinely lives in the large grazing animals of Africa. It is transported to humans only when a fly that has bitten an infected animal bites a human. The grazing animals in which the parasite is normally found are known as the **reservoir hosts** of the parasite. When the parasite gets into a human, it is still able to complete its life cycle. Because humans are not the normal home of the parasite, they are known as an **alternative host**. Nevertheless, the alternative host is often made ill and is sometimes killed by the parasite. Such is the case with sleeping sickness parasite, which can sometimes cause death to its human alternative host.

PARASITOLOGY

A parasite is defined as an organism that can live on or in another organism (a host) at the host's expense. Thus, a parasite in some way harms its host, either by competing with the host for nutrients or by slowly eating its host. A parasite that lives on the host, such as a flea or a skin bacterium, is called an ectoparasite. One that lives within the host, for example the *Plasmodium falciparum* parasite, is called an endoparasite. If the parasite cannot complete its life cycle outside of a host, it is called an obligate parasite.

An organism that normally lives on its own but can become parasitic if the opportunity arises is known as a facultative parasite. For example, the bacterium *Clostridium tetani*, the organism that causes tetanus, is a facultative parasite. Usually, this organism lives freely in the soil. But when it finds itself in dead tissue surrounding a deep puncture wound, as when someone steps on a rusty nail, it adjusts to living as a parasite.

Living on or in one's food source is ideal. Consequently, parasitism is a very successful lifestyle. Some organisms, such as nematodes, are extremely common endoparasites. They carry on their entire lives within their hosts. Such an organism is called a permanent parasite. Another type of parasite is one that visits only for a meal, such as a mosquito or horsefly. This is a temporary parasite.

Permanent endoparasites often make their hosts ill. It is not in their best interests to kill their host. Doing so may kill the parasite as well. Some parasites avoid this problem by abandoning their host, possibly causing its death in the process. Some flatworms that parasitize snails are an example of such an endoparasite-host relationship. Other parasites cannot abandon their host; however, they do shed their eggs before they die, thus ensuring the survival of their offspring and future generations of their species.

In the case of malaria, humans who are partially immune to the disease appear to be the reservoir host. Nonimmune humans act like the alternative hosts. The mosquito plays two roles. It is the vector, the means of transport from host to host. However, the parasite also needs the mosquito to complete its life cycle. That makes the mosquito a necessary part of the host-parasite cycle that is called the **intermediate host**.

Because the malaria life cycle involves more than one host, *Plasmodium* is more complex than many other parasites. Whenever a parasite shows an alternation of generations in separate hosts, it reproduces sexually in only one of them. That host is known as the **definitive host**. In the case of malaria, the definitive host is the mosquito. To summarize then, humans play the role of the reservoir host. Mosquitoes play the role of vector, alternative host, and definitive host.

As mentioned earlier, there are 50 or more species of *Plasmodium*, and only four of those species cause human malaria. Other species cause malaria in other animals, from reptiles to apes. Similarly, of the 400 or more species of *Anopheles* mosquitoes, perhaps 60 are capable of serving as alternative hosts and vectors for human malaria. There are no rules specifying that they can bite only humans, of course, and it would seem logical that human malaria could be spread to other animals. But human malaria usually does not infect other animals, other than *Plasmodium malariae*, which may affect apes or monkeys. The *Plasmodia* of human malaria are human parasites only.

It would seem equally logical that the *Plasmodia* that cause malaria in other organisms would infect humans rather regularly as well. However, whenever those parasites are passed to humans, they are immediately destroyed by the human immune system. Unlike the parasites that cause malaria in humans, they have not evolved the ability to avoid our immune system.

Finally, *Anopheles* mosquitoes do not spread the malaria parasites of other animals. They are spread by other genera of mosquitoes. Exactly how malaria became a human disease and how the *Anopheles* mosquito became the vector is unknown. The thinking on the subject that now exists is discussed in the next chapter.

The incubation period for *falciparum* malaria in human blood before symptoms begin to show is between 10 and 14 days, during which time the parasites undergo several reproductive cycles and their numbers grow. Once the population of parasites has become large enough, the rupture of the blood cells and the release of parasites (Figure 2.2) cause the victim to feel chills, one of the most common symptoms. The waste products released into the bloodstream trigger a reaction that several hours later culminates in the fever spikes associated with malaria.

Additionally, the removal of waste products from the blood by the kidneys causes a darkening of the urine, often referred to as blackwater urine. Headache, nausea, vomiting, joint pain, and body aches may accompany the fever. In the case of *Plasmodium falciparum*, symptoms can include brain infection, nervous dysfunction and confusion, progressive lethargy, seizures, and coma. Additionally, the victim can experience pulmonary edema (fluid in the lungs), dry cough, and anemia. Waste products can also lodge in the liver and spleen, where they cause damage. Eventually, however, the kidneys may fail. In up to 25 percent of cases, death will result.

In the non-*falciparum* malarias, the outlook is less dire. Death is rarely an outcome. Instead, the symptoms occur every two to three days and last from four to six hours each, and they occur less frequently over time. Symtoms include confusion, exhaustion, and extreme sweating (Figure 2.3). Recovery usually occurs in one to four weeks. When someone recovers from *falciparum* malaria, he or she usually does not have any lingering symptoms. However, the other types of malaria can become chronic. After recovery, the parasites can hide in the tissues and erupt years, even decades, later. Reoccurrences can occur for

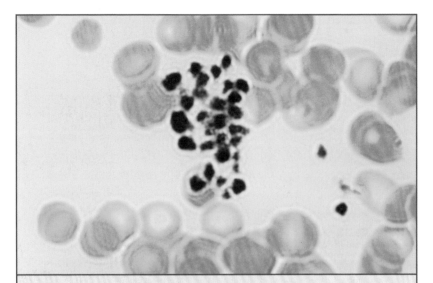

Figure 2.2 This photomicrograph shows *Plasmodium falciparum* reproductive cells being released from a ruptured red blood cell. These cells can now be picked up by a mosquito feeding on this person's blood. (© Biodisc/Visuals Unlimited)

as long as 50 years. Additionally, the disease can remain infective. There was fear that soldiers who had survived the malaria outbreak in the South Pacific during World War II would bring chronic malaria back to the United States and possibly start outbreaks here. There are, after all, several species of *Anopheles* mosquitoes that are common in North America, and at least some of them are compatible with *Plasmodium*.

THE VICTIMS

Mosquitoes are more likely to bite men than women, because mosquitoes are attracted to heat, and men give off more body heat than women do. This does not mean that mosquitoes will not bite women, however, including ones who are pregnant, and they will bite children as well, often preferentially

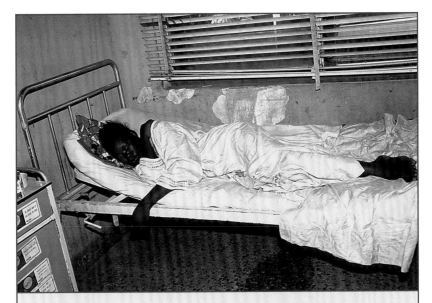

Figure 2.3   One of the common symptoms of malaria is lethargy and extreme fatigue. The woman shown here is in a clinic in Nigeria. (Courtesy WHO/Pierre Virot)

because children radiate more heat than adults. Malaria can be very serious in children and pregnant women, and *falciparum* malaria may develop into cerebral malaria in children. When this happens, red blood cells containing the parasite become isolated in the child's brain to the point that blood vessels may be blocked. Death can result. Death can also result to a fetus of a pregnant woman or to the pregnant woman herself. In Africa, where malaria is most common, such deaths are common.

THE SYMPTOMS OF MALARIA—IN SUMMARY

Before symptoms in someone infected with malaria begin to appear, there is an incubation period during which the parasites are quietly multiplying to levels where they begin to cause trouble. The incubation may be as short as a week, as is more often the case with *Plasmodium falciparum*, or as long as a month, which is more typical of the mild *P. malariae*. Once parasite levels in the blood are sufficiently high, symptoms begin to occur.

The classic malaria cycle lasts for about six to ten hours. It usually begins with intense chills and shivering as the victim develops a fever. This is followed by a period of elevated temperature, headaches, vomiting, and in the case of young children, seizures. Finally, there is a period of fatigue and heavy perspiration as body temperature returns to normal. In the case of quartan malaria, caused by *P. malariae*, the cycle repeats every four days. It occurs every third day in the case of the other three.

Unfortunately, the classic malaria cycle is not that often observed. The symptoms described in the previous paragraph do not always occur in a clear, sequential pattern; they may occur simultaneously, complicated by nausea, body aches, and/or general malaise. Initially, as with a number of infections, malaria may be mistaken for influenza. Later in the development of the disease, further complications occur, including neurological issues such as seizures or coma. In addition, the patient may show anemia and blackwater urine, as blood cells are destroyed and hemoglobin byproducts are removed from the bloodstream by the kidneys. These may occur with pulmonary edema, as fluid accumulates in the lungs, an enlarged spleen, and eventual kidney failure and death. [2]

Malaria does not always kill. *Plasmodium vivax* and *malariae* cause so-called benign malarias that are rarely fatal. Even *P. ovale* and *falciparum* are not always fatal, and they can become chronic, particularly in people with some natural immunity to malaria. In such cases, the parasites remain in the blood. An enlarged spleen is often symptomatic of this condition. *P. vivax* and *P. ovale* may sometimes appear to be cured, only to relapse months or even years later. In these infections, the parasites have retreated to the liver and become dormant, only to reappear at some later time. Following World War II, when malaria had pretty well been eradicated from the continental United States, and after the Korean and Vietnam wars, it was feared that soldiers infected while serving abroad would return with chronic or relapsing malarias and begin new cycles of infection in the United States. Fortunately, this did not happen.

3

The Origin, Evolution, and Ecology of Malaria

Long ago, in a temporary shelter on a hillside overlooking the north end of what is now called Lake Malawi, a shaman knelt helplessly by the side of his patient, a young woman who lay listlessly, sweat beading on her skin. A few hours earlier, she had been shivering violently. The fever had come on once the shivering had stopped and after she had passed black water. An older woman knelt by the sick woman's head, mopping her forehead with a damp cloth. The shaman knew nothing of this sickness, and he knew nothing of the leaves and vines in this area. The ones with which he was familiar and from which he could extract medicines did not grow here. The group had ventured into the region from the south less than a month earlier, driven out of their homes by the rains. Now one-third of their group was dying of the mysterious illness that had found them here.

The shaman rose to his feet and stepped outside, where the leader of the group looked at him expectantly. The shaman could only shake his head sadly. The leader nodded. The next day he would assemble the group and announce that they would leave, once again traveling to the north, away from the rains that had chased them from their home. Inside the shelter, a mosquito lit on the cheek of the dying young woman.

ORIGIN AND EVOLUTION

In the movie *Jurassic Park*, scientists were able to create dinosaurs by extracting DNA from blood in the stomachs of mosquitoes that had bitten dinosaurs. The mosquitoes had become trapped in tree resin while resting after their meal. When the resin hardened to amber, the mosquitoes became fossilized. The blood meal and DNA they had eaten remained intact. Sixty-five million years later, the scientists extracted the DNA from the fossilized mosquito and inserted it into an egg of a frog. A dinosaur hatched as a result.

Although the film's events might sound far-fetched, cloning technology may one day advance to the point where DNA extracted from a fossilized mosquito could be used to generate an extinct organism, but not a dinosaur. The dinosaurs became extinct over 65 million years ago. Mosquitoes have been around for less than half that time. How mosquitoes originated is not really known, but they have been biting ever since.

The origin of *Plasmodium* is also unknown. Some scientists believe that it originated in Africa as much as 30 million years ago, but others believe it originated in Asia before humans arrived there. The latter group cite the variety of malarias that exist there, in contrast to relatively few in Africa, as evidence of its Asian origin. Moreover, they note that certain Asian animal malarias are similar to human malarias, and some, such as the malaria of Malay irus monkeys caused by *Plasmodium knowlesi* and one of gibbons caused by *P. eylesi*, can be naturally transmitted to people. Oddly enough, malaria's ultimate ancestor may have been a free-living algae-like cell, because contemporary *Plasmodium* cells reportedly contain gene fragments for chlorophyll production.[1]

Definitive information on its evolution as a parasite is likewise lacking. Some scientists believe that *Plasmodium* was originally a parasite of other animals, possibly birds. One hypothesis states that malaria became a human parasite after humans domesticated birds. In fact, *Plasmodium falciparum* appears to be more closely related to bird malarias than monkey malarias, although chimpanzees harbor a malaria protozoan, *P. reichenowi*, that is genetically similar to *P. falciparum* but does not appear to infect humans. Whether this means that malaria occurred in the common ancestor of chimps and humans more than six million years ago or that each species was separately infected by similar *Plasmodia* more recently is unclear.

The other three species of human malarias are more closely related to monkey malarias, and it is remotely possible that some transmission of them between humans and monkeys can occur. Another hypothesis has it that *falciparum* malaria was accidentally transferred to people, perhaps by the blood of an infected bird contaminating an open sore on the hand of a person butchering it. Recent genetic studies on *P. falciparum* suggest that the modern form of the parasite may have originated as recently as 7,000 years ago, about the time agriculture originated in Africa. That it is the most virulent of the four human malarias supports thinking that it is the most recently evolved.[2, 3] However the transfer occurred, malaria became successful as a human parasite, particularly as people became more and more abundant and replaced other animals as they became extinct.

Illnesses of animals that are transferred to people are known as **zoonoses** (singular: zoonosis). Many common illnesses of humans, such as influenza, probably originated as zoonoses. Because *Plasmodium* is so specific to humans, however, it is doubtful that all malarias originated as zoonoses. More likely, they became parasites of our anthropoid (apelike) ancestors, evolving with them to become parasites of humans.

ECOLOGY OF MALARIA I:
The Life Cycle of the Vector

The ecology of malaria depends entirely on the life cycle of the *Anopheles* mosquito (Figure 3.1). The success of *Plasmodium* in completing its life cycle is intimately tied to the success of the *Anopheles* mosquito in completing its life cycle, which can be difficult. The mosquito's life is constantly in danger, and its lifespan is very short.

Mosquito Life Cycle

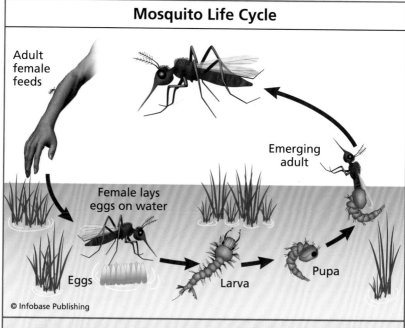

Adult female feeds

Emerging adult

Female lays eggs on water

Eggs

Larva

Pupa

© Infobase Publishing

Figure 3.1 This illustration shows the mosquito life cycle. After taking a blood meal, female mosquitoes lay eggs on the surface of shallow, still water. These eggs hatch into larvae. Larvae grow into pupae, which develop into adult mosquitoes, which leave the water to hunt for food.

A mosquito's life is critically dependent on water, where the female lays her eggs. She can lay eggs in bodies as small as birdbaths, drainage ditches, and discarded paper cups. Humans have contributed to the creation of breeding areas, which will be discussed later in the chapter. In colder regions, the eggs may remain dormant over the winter. The eggs hatch when the water warms in the spring. After larvae hatch from the eggs (Figure 3.2), they live suspended from the surface of the water, breathe through an air tube, and eat organic matter, which they filter through their mouthparts. Known as "wrigglers" because of their swimming motion, the larvae swim toward shelter if

Figure 3.2 After a mosquito egg hatches, the offspring is called a larva, shown here. This larva will molt four times before becoming a pupa. (© Biodisc/Visuals Unlimited)

anything disturbs them. Because the wrigglers breathe air, they can survive in stagnant or polluted water that is low in oxygen. Many larvae are eaten by predacious insects and small fish. Those that survive grow. Each larva sheds its skin four times, a process known as molting. Then, it changes into a pupa. The pupa, known as a tumbler, swims freely, but remains vulnerable to predators. Once it metamorphoses into an adult, it leaves the water and flies to a nearby tree to rest and gather its energy. In the air the mosquito is vulnerable to bats, swallows, dragonflies, and any other flying predator. Mosquitoes that escape flying predators run the risk of flying into a spider's web. Those that make it to a tree are often eaten by ants or hunting spiders. Very few mosquitoes, perhaps fewer than 1 in 10, live long enough to bite anybody. Of those that do, only the female bites. The male feeds on plant nectar. Female mosquitoes mate only once in their lives. Mating usually occurs shortly after they emerge as adults (Figure 3.3).

FINDING THEIR MEALS

One of life's more annoying petty experiences is to lie in bed at night with mosquitoes humming in your ears. You cannot see them to swat them, but they seem to know exactly where you are. Furthermore, why are they attracted to your ears?

Mosquitoes do not see well during the daytime. They can see movement and are attracted to it. They can also see an object that contrasts with its background. However, they are especially attracted to the carbon dioxide (CO_2) we exhale, to the warmth that radiates from our bodies, and to the moisture that we emit through perspiration and respiration. A mosquito can sense the CO_2 in our breath from as far as 100 feet (35 meters) away. In addition, our blood carries heat from deep within our bodies, heat that is radiated by our skin to keep us from overheating. Mosquitoes can "see" this heat as infrared light through sensors on their antennae, and they are attracted to it. Because our ears are highly vascularized, which means that they are richly supplied with blood vessels, they radiate a lot of heat. Consequently, in a dark room, a person's ears look like a buffet table to a mosquito. Ironically, mosquitoes are blind to the ultraviolet "bug" lights that many people suspend in their yards. The lights are effective against some flying insects such as moths, which are attracted to ultraviolet lights, but not mosquitoes. Finally, there are chemicals in perspiration that mosquitoes can smell. People who perspire heavily attract more mosquitoes than do people who do not sweat readily, because both the moisture they give off and the chemicals in sweat attract mosquitoes.

Only the female mosquito bites. (Males live on plant nectar.) She requires a meal of blood to produce her eggs but risks being swatted as she gets it. The female mosquito drinks two or more times her weight in blood. After feeding, she flies to a vertical surface, such as a wall, and digests her meal. At this time,

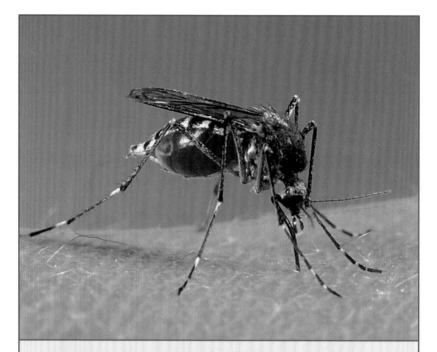

Figure 3.3   Only female mosquitoes feed on blood; here you can see that this mosquito's abdomen is engorged with her blood meal. The energy from the blood meal enables the female mosquito to lay her eggs. (Courtesy Agricultural Research Service (ARS), U.S. Department of Agriculture)

she again may be vulnerable to hunting spiders or other insects that may also be nearby. One East African spider preferentially preys on mosquitoes that are engorged with human blood. The jumping spider *Evarcha culicivora* of Kenya and Uganda appears to relish human blood, but it is unable to drink it directly. Instead, it gets blood indirectly by specifically selecting resting mosquitoes that have recently bitten someone.[4]

One problem a mosquito must solve is to prevent her victim's blood from coagulating as she feeds. She accomplishes this by injecting an anticoagulant into the tissue surrounding the bite. The welt and itch that accompanies a mosquito bite is an allergic reaction to the anticoagulant.

ECOLOGY OF MALARIA II:
Distribution and Transmission

Mosquitoes in general, and *Anopheles* mosquitoes in particular, have adapted to virtually every environment on Earth where fresh water is available. Consequently, malaria has become a cosmopolitan disease, meaning that it occurs worldwide. However, it is most problematic in Africa, especially south of the Sahara Desert, where it kills one child every 30 seconds on average. The mosquito present there, *Anopheles gambiae*, is well adapted to coexisting with people. It prefers human blood, and it feeds by day, when people are outside. Moreover, it can breed in as little water as the amount that accumulates in a hoof print after a rain; virtually all other species of mosquitoes need larger volumes. *Anopheles gambiae* typically bites every other day. It takes only 12 days for *Plasmodium falciparum* to complete the stage of its life cycle that occurs in mosquitoes. Roughly 30 percent of all mosquitoes that have bitten a person infected with malaria live long enough to bite a second victim and thus spread the disease. That may not seem like much, but mosquitoes multiply by the thousands. The commonality of malaria testifies to the survival success of those mosquitoes.

ECOLOGY OF MALARIA III:
Persistence and Tolerance of the Disease

Immunity to any disease often results from exposure to that disease. This applies to malaria but not perfectly. Human malarias appear to have evolved the ability to avoid the human immune system, and humans cannot develop a complete immunity to malaria as we can with, for example, smallpox. It is possible, however, to develop a partial immunity to malaria. In this case, a survivor would remain infected with the parasites, but he or she would not show symptoms of the disease. Moreover, he or

she could survive to reproduce and pass the immunity to a suc-
ceeding generation.

The ability to generate resistance to a disease is initially
genetic—that is, people must have the genes that will allow
them to develop a resistance. Those people who do not are
more likely to die. As a result, those who are resistant are more
likely to survive and pass on their resistance to their offspring.
Consequently, a population that is constantly exposed to
malaria is most likely to be resistant. The disadvantage of that
is that resistant people can serve as reservoirs for the parasite.
For example, malaria is now common in Sri Lanka. Itinerant

SICKLE CELL DISEASE

Sickle cell disease probably originated in Africa. This may
explain why in the United States, it is most abundant among
African Americans, affecting perhaps one in 400. However,
sickle cell disease also occurs in the Middle East and around
the Mediterranean Sea. It may have been brought there by
African slaves. Any of those slaves or their descendents who
later married into the native populations could have started
spreading the gene among them. With the protection it offered
against malaria, it would have easily survived any place where
malaria was present.

Sickle cell disease is an inherited blood disorder that
affects hemoglobin, the oxygen-carrying component of blood.
Hemoglobin is made from protein, which is made of smaller
components called amino acids. There are four protein chains
in a hemoglobin molecule. In one of the chains, an amino
acid is missing, substituted with another amino acid. The
result is a hemoglobin molecule that is misshapen. The blood
cell carrying that hemoglobin ends up misshapen as well.

Sickle cell disease causes a number of pathological problems. Sickle cell hemoglobin does not carry oxygen as well as

construction workers, subsistence farmers, and others without permanent housing are sufficiently resistant to the disease to survive and reproduce while infected with it. They continue to be the reservoir in that country. It is ironic that a population's resistance to malaria requires ongoing infection. If malaria is eliminated from a population and then reintroduced after a couple of generations, everybody is vulnerable. An epidemic may result. Equally ironic is that when resistant people travel to areas where malaria is not present but compatible mosquitoes exist, they can take the disease with them and introduce it. This too can result in an epidemic.

normal hemoglobin. In addition, it can cause heart enlargement, enlargement of the extremities, disturbed blood flow and blockage of small blood vessels, leg ulcers, susceptibility to infection, and early death.

The heredity of sickle cell disease follows the laws of simple dominance. To have the disease, one must inherit two recessive genes, one from each parent. Such an individual is said to be homozygous for the trait. Someone who inherits the gene from only one parent is described a being heterozygous. If two heterozygous individuals have a child together, there is a one in four chance that the child will be homozygous (i.e., will have the disease).

Treating sickle cell anemia is difficult. Currently, there are no genetic therapies. Antibiotics help prevent infection and, therefore, save many lives.

A screening test for carriers is available. Relatives of sickle cell victims who suspect they may have the disease can have the test. If a couple finds that they are both carriers, they can then decide whether or not to take their chances on having children of their own or adopting.

Perhaps most ironic is the fact that there is a population of people that is truly immune to malaria, but they pay a heavy price for it. These are the people who have or carry a genetic condition known as sickle cell disease, sometimes called sickle cell anemia. This is an inherited disorder where the hemoglobin in the blood is shaped differently from normal hemoglobin (Figure 3.4). Someone who inherits this condition from both parents has so much abnormal hemoglobin that his or her red blood cells are distorted. Sickle cell hemoglobin does not carry oxygen well. The individual with the disease may suffer any number of symptoms, including pain, fever, and damage to organs. Without medical treatment, victims of this disease die young, often in childhood. However, someone who inherits the trait from only one parent has largely normal hemoglobin and is spared the worst consequences. He or she can live a relatively normal life, although he or she cannot live at very high altitudes. He or she is immune to malaria, however, because the *Plasmodium* parasite cannot survive in the modified red blood cell. Consequently, sickle cell disease provides persistent survival value to people who have it. It is a genetic protection against malaria, but because it can cause death in some circumstances, it is an imperfect solution.

Another inherited blood disorder that may offer protection against severe malaria is the thalassemias (singular: thalassemia), a group of distortions of the hemoglobin molecule that, like sickle cell disease, may compromise the malaria parasite's ability to utilize it. Reportedly the most common genetic disorders of humans, it occurs frequently in some African populations, and it may be one reason that many of the children who develop malaria do not die as a result. Thalassemia causes anemia that ranges from mild to more severe, but unlike *falciparum* malaria, it is rarely fatal.[5]

SPREAD AND PERSISTENCE OF THE DISEASE

Even though malaria is considered to be a tropical disease, it has occurred in temperate and even subpolar areas where *Anopheles*

Figure 3.4 Sickle cell anemia is a disease that causes blood cells to become misshapen, often looking like "sickles," as in this micrograph. Sickle cells cannot carry oxygen as efficiently as normal blood cells. The disease also causes poor blood flow throughout the body and can result in death. Interestingly, people who have sickle cell anemia are resistant to malaria. (© Biodisc/Visuals Unlimited)

mosquitoes exist. It is possible that an infected mosquito can be transported to an area where malaria is nonexistent and begin an epidemic. Malaria may have been transported from Africa to Brazil this way. Similarly, the so-called tiger mosquito of the South Pacific, the vector for dengue fever, has recently been "shipped" to the Western Hemisphere. More commonly, however, an infected person travels into an area where there is no malaria, an *Anopheles* mosquito bites him or her, and the epidemic begins. Malaria has been transported all over the world.

Human activities have often ensured malaria's survival. Construction areas, for example, have provided abundant breeding grounds. Mosquitoes now breed in places such as eaves, troughs, birdbaths, drainage ditches, leech ponds, and poorly tended swimming pools. Discarded tires and other kinds of litter that can hold water have provided additional breeding grounds. Items as common as pottery vessels can also serve as a breeding ground. The construction of ponds and reservoirs, even backyard garden ponds, provide even more breeding grounds.

Anopheles mosquitoes typically breed in permanent bodies of water, although *Anopheles gambiae* may be the conspicuous exception to this rule. Construction of permanent water bodies contributed to the population growth of these mosquitoes and their subsequent spread of malaria when the disease arrived in regions they inhabited. Thus, malaria may have made its way as far north as upstate New York, where it found a compatible mosquito and caused havoc during the construction of the Erie Canal. One bit of good fortune, however, was that *Plasmodium falciparum*, the most deadly form of malaria, was unable to survive the winters there. Even when an infected mosquito could survive the winter weather, *Plasmodium falciparum* was unable to become dormant. It usually died before the mosquito could start biting again in the spring. Still, malaria in its different forms managed to make its way around the world, and its impact on history was major.

4

The Discovery
of *Plasmodium*

After the War of 1812, the British government decided to construct a canal in its colony of Canada from Ottawa to Kingston. This canal would run in part along the Rideau River to create a waterway completely within Canadian territory rather than to rely on the St. Lawrence River, which the British felt was vulnerable to American attack. Construction on the canal began in 1826, and every summer workers, their wives, and children took ill. In 1831, canal contractor John Redpath described:

> . . . the exceeding unhealthiness of the place from which cause all engaged in it suffered much from lake fever and fever & ague [fever with chills], and it has also retarded the work for about three months each year. I caught the disease both the first [1828] and second year, missed the third, but this year had a severe attack of Lake Fever— which kept me to bed for two months and nearly two months more before I was fit for active service, as nothing can compensate for the worse of health so no inducement whatever would stimulate one to a similar undertaking.

The malaria that affected the Rideau workers was *P. vivax* malaria, usually a nonfatal form. However, the workers suffered from concurrent illnesses such as dysentery, and the two together weakened them beyond their tolerance.[1]

Some scientists believe that malaria may have originated in Africa around 30 million years ago. Human malaria perhaps evolved into its along with our anthropoid and early human ancestors, although nobody really knows when. There is no record of its presence in Europe until the first century A.D., when it was first recorded in Rome. It has been hypothesized that malaria was brought to Rome by Roman troops returning from Africa or by the African slaves they brought with them. However it got there, an *Anopheles* mosquito that was capable of spreading the disease inhabited the swamps around Rome and was waiting for it.

Another hypothesis has it that malaria existed on the Italian peninsula for centuries before the first century A.D. Its presence may have kept invaders from defeating Rome. For example, Hannibal's army from Carthage nearly succeeded in attacking the city of Rome in 218–201 B.C., but was stopped north of Rome, and some historians maintain that it was malaria, at least in part, that stopped them. Whichever hypothesis, if either, is correct, malaria in Rome did periodically cause the deaths of non-Italians, including invading armies. The native Italians, in contrast, who were constantly exposed to and probably continually infected with malaria, were able to maintain some resistance to the disease. Moreover, after the Roman Empire fell, the population of the Italian peninsula continued to be protected by the endemic malaria. Although Rome may have been defeated, invaders never occupied the Italian peninsula. It was not until the twentieth century when Benito Mussolini, the dictator of Italy from 1922 to 1943, had the swamps around Rome drained that malaria was finally brought under control.

Although malaria may have protected Rome, it may also have contributed to its downfall. People infected with malaria are often lethargic. Lethargy is said to have characterized Rome later in the history of the empire. By the fourth century A.D., Roman legions were made up mostly of Germanic tribes, not Roman Italians. Ironically, Rome is said to have lost more than 40,000 of those legionnaires in Scotland to malaria during its campaign in the British Isles. When Rome did finally fall to the barbarians, the conquerors failed to occupy the Italian peninsula.

After the fall of Rome, European armies remained at home, for the most part, with the Crusades being the conspicuous exception. Beginning with the voyages of Columbus, however, Europeans once again started claiming territory throughout the rest of the world. They established colonies throughout the Americas and much of Asia fairly easily, but not in Africa. Indeed, the colonization of Africa may have been delayed for 300 years by the endemic diseases of the continent, including malaria and yellow fever. In fact, some of Africa never came under European dominance because of malaria.

Malaria even interfered with European colonization in parts of Southeast Asia. For example, malaria was well established in New Guinea, especially in the lowland areas. It inhibited European settlement there. In contrast, Indonesians, who had been exposed to malaria for a long time and thus had immunity to the disease, had no trouble moving into New Guinea. The Europeans also had problems elsewhere in Asia. For example, the British lost many soldiers in India to malaria.

It is generally believed that malaria did not exist in the Western Hemisphere before Columbus discovered the Americas. It is also believed that malaria was brought to the United States by the Spaniards and by the European slave trade. Whether or not these theories are correct, it is likely that maritime traders brought malaria to the Americas from Europe and Africa, probably by infected African slaves who brought this and other African diseases with them and by fast ships that carried infected mosquitoes to South America. Once malaria was brought to the Americas, it was spread throughout the New World by North and South American *Anopheles* mosquitoes that bit Africans and Europeans indiscriminately. Indeed, in the 1870s, malaria and yellow fever contributed to the failure of an attempt by the French to build a canal across Panama. Additionally, malaria delayed the exploration and colonization of much of what is now Brazil.

The spread of malaria throughout the United States and elsewhere in the Americas was facilitated by a number of ironic twists. First, the organizers in Europe who were responsible for the decisions that brought malaria to the United States never left Europe. They never had to suffer the consequences of their decisions.

Second, the conversion of North America to a new Europe contributed to the spread of malaria in the United States. As North America was developed, agriculture became very important. Some of it, however, involved constructing irrigation ditches, water catchments, and even small ponds. Such structures caused standing water that provided ideal breeding conditions for *Anopheles* mosquitoes.

MALARIA AS A CURE

One oddity in medicine is the use of one disease to treat another. In 1887, Julius Wagner-von Jauregg, an Austrian psychiatrist, suggested that malaria could be used to treat syphilis. Theoretically, the high temperatures caused by malaria fevers would kill the syphilis bacteria. The idea did not initially catch on because of the dangers inherent in malaria infection and because by 1917, quinine was available for treatment of malaria. Von Jauregg did use malaria to treat syphilis successfully in Austria after World War I using *Plasmodium knowlesi*, a parasite of Malayan irus monkeys that caused a self-limiting fever in humans. *P. knowlesi* generated high enough fevers in humans to kill the syphilis bacteria, but the malaria it caused required no treatment. Prior to World War I he had used *P. vivax*. Whether the elevated temperature or some other reason nobody knows cured the syphilis, the treatment did work, and von Jauregg was awarded the 1927 Nobel Prize in medicine for his work. Today, however, as long as syphilis bacteria remain susceptible to antibiotics, it is unlikely that malaria will be used to cure it.

Agriculture was not the only change in North America that exposed immigrants to malaria. Other construction projects did as well. For example, the first important inland waterway constructed in North America was the Erie Canal. Built between 1817 and 1825, it connected the Hudson River in New York City to Lake Erie at Buffalo. The canal allowed commerce from New York City and the rest of the East Coast to upstate New York and midwestern cities that were on Lake Erie. West of Syracuse, the land through which the canal was slated to be built was very swampy. Currently, that region is the Montezuma National Wildlife Refuge, named most likely for the Aztec chief. At that time, the land was a mess of standing water and a mosquito hatchery. *Anopheles* mosquitoes are common in upstate New York. The introduction of malaria to the region, probably by an infected canal worker, was all it took to start a small epidemic. Many workers reportedly became ill and died with malaria during the construction of the canal. The illness may have delayed the completion of the project. A similar story has been reported about the construction of the Ohio Canal near Cleveland.

Upstate New York and northern Ohio were not the only places in the United States affected by malaria. It was fairly common in the South, particularly in New Orleans, before World War II. Immigrant Irish laborers who worked in the swamps around New Orleans in the nineteenth century were especially victimized by the disease. Irish laborers working on public works projects in Boston during the nineteenth century also consistently encountered malaria.

For most of history, infections caused the largest number of deaths. Even during wars, more soldiers died from infected wounds than from the injuries themselves. World War II was the first war in which that was not the case, largely because of antibiotics. Most of the infections spread during war were bacterial, against which antibiotics worked. Malaria, however, was a conspicuous exception. It is caused by a protozoan, and the standard antibiotics had no effect on it. Moreover, in the South Pacific and East Asia, malaria continued to kill more Allied soldiers than battle did. Bringing malaria under control was crucial to the Allied victory in the South Pacific, and it continued to play an important role in world politics following the war.

The end of World War II brought about sweeping changes in the balance of world political power, which saw the planet divided essentially into two hostile camps. One, the Western Alliance, was dominated by the United States with the principal support of the nations of Western Europe. The other was dominated by Russia and the countries it absorbed as a result of World War II. Both camps tried to win influence with the rest of the world. Part of the strategy of the Western Alliance was to raise the living standards of the countries they were courting, and one part of their strategy was to provide medical aid. In the case of malaria, it was believed that the best strategy was prevention by controlling the vector. By that time, **DDT** (dichloro-diphenyl-trichloroethane), a potent insecticide, was available. DDT appeared to be effective against mosquitoes. By 1958, because of the use of DDT, victory against malaria was declared. In fact, medical schools stopped teaching about the disease. Subsequently, research on the disease was stopped, which turned out to be a big mistake. Malaria had receded, but it had not disappeared.

THE DISCOVERY OF *PLASMODIUM*

Among the reasons why malaria had such an impact on history was that until fairly recently people had no idea what caused the disease, nor how it was spread. As widespread as malaria is today, it is easy to overlook how much progress had been made against it during the past 150 years. It took almost 2,000 years for the cause of malaria to be discovered. In 1880, the French Army surgeon Charles Louis Alphonse Laveran (1845–1922) discovered the *Plasmodium* protozoan (Figure 4.1). Laveran,

Figure 4.1 Charles Louis Alphonse Laveran discovered the *Plasmodium* parasite, which causes malaria. He was awarded the Nobel Prize in medicine in 1907 for his work on this parasite, as well as his work on uncovering the role played by other disease-causing bacteria. (© The Nobel Foundation)

who also described the protozoan that causes sleeping sickness, was convinced that mosquitoes were responsible for spreading malaria. Laveran's discovery was met with initial skepticism, even disdain. As a military physician, he was not considered to have the scientific credentials of the researchers of his time, and his ability to sketch the parasites in blood did not match his ability to see them. Moreover, the microscopes of the time were crude, and for other researchers lacking his sharp eyesight the parasites remained elusive. Once the optics on microscopes were improved, however, others saw the malaria parasites in blood and accepted Laveran's discovery, as a result of which he was awarded the Nobel Prize in medicine in 1907.

Sir Patrick Manson (1844–1922), a Scottish physician, confirmed in 1900 that mosquitoes spread malaria. He accomplished this by allowing infected mosquitoes to bite volunteers. Manson had earlier discovered the worm that causes elephantiasis, a disease that causes swelling of the limbs, and that the worm was spread by mosquitoes. This discovery may have given him the idea about malaria. Manson initially thought that the mosquito was a passive transmitter of *Plasmodium,* as it was with the elephantiasis worm. He believed that people got malaria by drinking water in which infected mosquitoes had died after laying their eggs.

The third link in the chain of discovery of malaria was Sir Donald Ross (1857–1932), another British physician and something of an unlikely hero in this saga. He originally wanted to be a poet rather than a physician. However, after meeting Manson, he became an ardent researcher. Ross discovered the malaria parasite in the gut of a mosquito. Indeed, it was Ross's discovery that gave Manson the idea to have infected mosquitoes bite volunteers. It was Ross who was credited with confirming that *Anopheles* was the villain in human malaria. He had initially discovered the role of mosquitoes in spreading bird malaria. He found the infective form in the mosquito's salivary gland. The real credit for the

Figure 4.2 Sir Patrick Manson. (U. S. National Institutes of Health/National Library of Medicine)

discovery of *Anopheles* as the human vector may, however, be due to his Indian field assistant, Muhammed Bux, who captured the mosquitoes.

BRINGING MALARIA UNDER CONTROL

Once the cause and transmission of malaria had become understood, steps could be taken to interrupt the cycle of the disease and reduce its impact. Swamps could be drained, windows could be screened, and care could be taken to remove standing water from structures on the ground. Even specific poisons could be used. Indeed, using these measures eventually brought malaria under control and almost totally eliminated it. Unfortunately, "almost" was not enough, and malaria has rebounded, as will be described in later chapters.

It is, of course, impossible to speculate what the world would have been like if malaria had never evolved or spread. However, it seems reasonable to conclude that history would have been different.

5

Diagnosis and Treatment

One legend has it that among the first Europeans to be cured of malaria by quinine was the Countess of Chinchón, Señora Ana de Osorio, wife of the fourth Count of Chinchón of Spain in 1829. She became ill with malaria soon after arriving in Lima, Peru. The governor of the Peruvian city of Loxa, Don Juan López, had recently suffered from what may have been malaria and was cured by missionaries who had learned from natives with whom they had lived about the power of cinchona bark. Don Juan López wrote to the count offering to provide cinchona bark to the countess. Summoned to do so, he and the count's physician administered the remedy and the countess recovered. The legend goes on to say that it was the countess and the physician, Juan de Vega, who brought cinchona bark to Europe when they returned.

DIAGNOSIS

Imagine someone going to a hospital emergency room with fever and severe headache. Physicians would perform the usual array of tests. Most of them, other than blood cell count, would probably come out normal. The physicians would most likely find this confusing. They might call on specialists for help. The patient's headaches might be a reason to call a neurologist, for example. Most American physicians would be slow to diagnose malaria, simply because they have never seen it. Consequently, someone who shows up in an American hospital emergency room with a case of malaria stands a great chance of being misdiagnosed. Of course, if the patient in question has recently been in a tropical country and the doctor thinks to ask about that, the odds of diagnosing malaria improve. There is still a good chance, however, that a diagnosis of malaria would not occur to most American physicians. Most have too little experience with the disease to suggest it.

One would think that the symptoms of malaria, including chills, fever, and blackwater urine, would be a good indication of the disease. However, there are a number of other diseases, such as severe nephritis, that could cause the same symptoms. The only way to positively diagnose malaria is by examining the patient's blood. A sample of blood is spread into a thin film on a glass slide, and the slide is examined under a microscope. If *Plasmodium* is found to be present in any of the blood cells, then malaria is confirmed.

There are several other ways malaria can be diagnosed. For example, there is a "dipstick" method, in which a chemically sensitive strip of paper that detects parasite proteins is dipped in blood. A specific color change indicates the presence of the malarial proteins. There is also a technique called polymerase chain reaction (PCR), where DNA fragments are replicated to increase the quantity of identifiable *Plasmodium* genes in a blood sample. This is an extremely accurate test, but it is expensive and it requires specialized laboratories.[1]

Past or chronic malaria can be detected with the indirect fluorescent antibody test (IFA). This uses specimens of *Plasmodium* stages normally found in the blood. These are mixed with specific patient blood samples. If malaria-specific immune proteins, **antibodies**, are present, they bond with complementary **antigens**, molecules on the *Plasmodium* cell surface, forming a complex. Additional specific antibodies are then added to the mixture. These adhere to the malaria antibodies if present, and the existence of a past or chronic malaria infection is confirmed when the mixture is examined under a fluorescence microscope. The parasites appear as fluorescent green bodies.

A test that is available in kits and can be done in the field to detect the presence of malaria antigens or antibodies is the enzyme-linked immunosorbent assay (ELISA). Blood serum, plasma with the clotting proteins removed, is mixed with malaria antigens. A color indicator is then added, and a specific color change indicates the presence of malaria antibodies in the serum.

There are other biochemical tests to detect parasite chemicals as well. The examination of blood films, however, remains the standard means of diagnosis.

TREATMENT

The first treatment of malaria was with quinine, a compound isolated from the bark of the *Cinchona* tree of South America (Figure 5.1). Sometimes it is still the most effective treatment available.

The first people to use *Cinchona* medically were the Indians of Peru, who used finely ground bark to treat fever. It was reasonable, therefore, for them to try to treat the fevers of malaria with ground cinchona bark. This treatment proved to be successful. Technically, quinine does not cure malaria because it does not kill all species of the parasite, but it kills enough of them to cure many people. Additionally, it does not kill at all stages of the *Plasmodium* life cycle. However, quinine can control the fevers of malaria and provide relief from the suffering. In certain areas, such as parts of South America, where newer malarial drugs are ineffective, unavailable, or too expensive, quinine is still used to treat malaria. Usually quinine is given orally. In severe cases, where kidney failure or coma has occurred, it is given intravenously.

The first synthetic antimalarial medication was developed in Germany during the 1930s. It was called Atabrine and it was used by the U.S. troops in World War II. More medications were developed during World War II. These include chloroquine, and doxycycline.

A number of antimalarial medications are used in combination. The treatment regimen varies according to the medication being used. For example, quinine, as quinine sulfate, is used in combination with the antibiotic doxycycline for seven days to treat *falciparum* malaria. It is effective, but it causes a

Figure 5.1 The *Cinchona* tree is the source for quinine. It is native to South America, where the native peoples used an extract containing quinine to treat fever. Quinine can be found in the bark, the roots, and the branches of the tree. (© Gianni Dagli Orti/CORBIS)

number of side effects, including hearing problems, nausea, and depression. A synthetic version of quinine, chloroquine, was developed and is now generally available. It is better tolerated than quinine, but *Plasmodium* in some parts of the world have become resistant to it.

Alternatively, a medication called Malarone®, a commercial combination of drugs, can be used for three days. The drug is effective, but very expensive. A third possibility is mefloquine for two days. The disadvantage of using mefloquine is that it causes severe stomach upset and has to be administered with a medication that prevents vomiting. Another combination drug is Fansidar®, which is made by combining sulfadoxine and pyramethamine, both of which inhibit chemical reactions in the blood stages of the malaria parasite and are considered effective against *P. falciparum*. This medication is used principally as a treatment, not a prevention. As seems to be the case with all other malarial medications, there are side effects to Fansidar. It seems to be particularly hard on the kidneys, and in can trigger allergic and other reactions. In addition, there are areas in Southeast Asia, South America, and central Africa where there is resistance to the drug. However, it is another weapon clinicians can use in some parts of the world.

The impetus to develop synthetic antimalarial drugs occurred during World War II, when the Japanese cut off the Allied supply of quinine from *Cinchona* after they conquered the South Pacific. Fortunately, chemists in Allied countries quickly developed synthetic substitutes.

Some of the medications that are used to treat malaria are also useful in preventing malaria. Unfortunately, some malaria medications are becoming less effective. The ineffectiveness of these medications may prove to be a problem in the future.

DRUG INEFFECTIVENESS

Any time we look at a group of people, we can easily identify differences among individuals. To *Plasmodium*, however, all people look pretty much alike. Similarly, any person looking at a culture of *Plasmodium* will not see much difference among individual parasites. Differences do exist, however. One difference is the susceptibility to various medications.

Plasmodium protozoa vary in their susceptibility to quinine. The variation in susceptibility can be explained as follows: Suppose enough quinine is added to a culture of *Plasmodium* to kill 99 percent of the parasites. The surviving organisms are less susceptible to the antibiotic than the ones that died. The survivors are then allowed to reproduce until their numbers equal those in the original culture. It is likely

CINCHONA TREES

Cinchona is a genus of South American trees that belong to the family of plants known as the Rubiaceae, or madders. In the 1630s, Catholic missionaries in Peru observed the native people using bark from *Cinchona* trees to relieve fevers and as a muscle relaxant to relieve nighttime leg cramps. *Cinchona* trees were not known as a cure for malaria at the time because malaria was not yet recognized, if indeed it was present, in South America. Within 10 years, the use of *Cinchona* trees to relieve fever had spread to Europe. Its eventual use in the treatment of malaria possibly resulted from first using it to relieve the fevers of malaria.

Quinine, the compound in *Cinchona* that is effective against malaria, is present in the root, branches, and bark of the tree. It is from the bark that quinine has traditionally been extracted and used medically. The bark was stripped off the trees and powdered. The use of *Cinchona* bark was so popular that trees were stripped without thought to conservation. Consequently, by the 1850s, the trees were becoming scarce and the price of the bark climbed. Perhaps pharmaceutical producers became concerned about extinction of the trees and the consequent loss of quinine to treat malaria. The trees were that the survivors would pass on their resistance to their off-spring. It is also possible that gene mutations would occur that might make one individual even more resistant to the drug. This mutant would then pass on its resistance. Consequently, although the same amount of quinine that killed 99 percent of the original culture might not leave the newer culture untouched, it would kill fewer than it did in the original. The mutant individuals would require an even stronger preparation of quinine to be killed. This resistance can happen when a patient is given too little of an antibiotic, the patient does not take all of the medication, or the treatment is too short to kill

subsequently introduced in Asia for cultivation, more likely for economic than conservationist reasons.

By 1820, scientists had learned how to extract quinine and cinchonine, another compound that is effective against malaria, from the bark rather than using powdered bark. This continued to be the practice during World War II, even though quinine had been synthesized by the 1930s. However, the Japanese occupation of the East Indies during the Second World War cut off the Allies from their sources of quinine in Asia. Consequently, it became a matter of necessity that they developed synthetic medications for malaria.

Cinchona trees continue to grow in South America today. There are three major species of the tree. *Cinchona officinalis* grows in the Andes Mountains in Ecuador. *Cinchona calisaya* grows in Bolivia. *Cinchona succirubra* grows in Bolivia and Peru. Undoubtedly each species is not restricted to the country with which it is mentioned. There may be other species of *Cinchona* as well. Although there are other types of trees from which quinine can be extracted, *Cinchona* has been the major source of quinine, and its impact on history cannot be denied.

Quinine

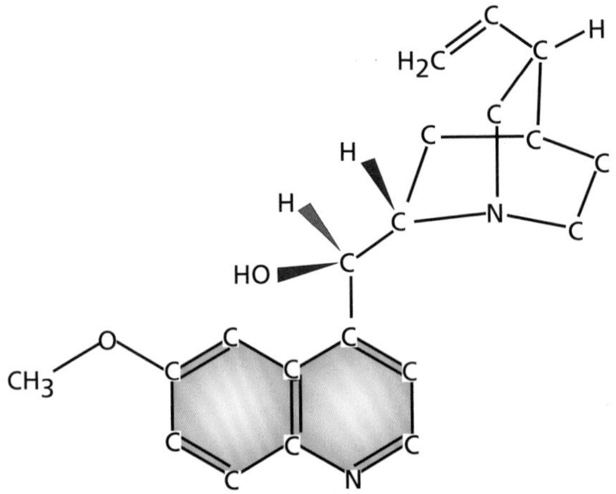

© Infobase Publishing

Figure 5.2   The molecular structure of quinine is shown here. Quinine helps to alleviate the high fevers associated with malaria. Quinine kills *Plasmodium* at some, but not all, stages of its life cycle. For this reason, it cannot be considered a true cure for the disease.

the entire parasite population. The drug will selectively allow resistant members to survive and pass on their resistance. Several rounds of this can end up leading to the evolution of totally resistant parasites.

This situation has happened with bacteria that have become resistant to drugs like penicillin. It is also happening with *Plasmodium* that are becoming resistant to quinine, chloroquine, and other antimalarial medications. Indeed, in Africa, India, and Southeast Asia, most strains of *falciparum* malaria are resistant to chloroquine. Worse, in Cambodia and Thailand, there are some types of *falciparum* that appear to be resistant to all antimalarial drugs.

HERBAL TREATMENT

Recently, there has been a lot of interest in herbal medicines. By definition, an herbal medication is one that is extracted from a plant. For example, a daisy-like plant by the name of echinacea has been reported to be effective in shortening the duration and reducing the intensity of the common cold. Another plant, the saw palmetto, common to the southeastern United States, has been shown to be beneficial for male urinary health.

By that definition, quinine could be considered an herbal medication because it was isolated from a tree. In general, herbal medicines are not commonly used in the United States. Elsewhere, such as in China, for example, herbal medicines are used to treat malaria. One herb that is particularly effective is a compound known as artemisinin or sometimes artesunate.

DOXYCYCLINE

Although doxycycline is effective in treating malaria, its principal use has been as a treatment for bacterial infections. Most antibacterial antibiotics, for example penicillin, ciprofloxine, and streptomycin, are ineffective against protozoa.

Doxycycline is part of the tetracycline group of antibiotics. It affects bacteria by interrupting protein synthesis, thus stopping their growth and allowing body defenses to work against them. It is also effective against a number of infections, including Lyme disease, some gastrointestinal disorders, and urinary tract infections.

There are a few disadvantages to using doxycycline, however. For example, it can cause discoloration of teeth in growing children. Additionally, it can cause gastrointestinal distress, such as diarrhea and nausea. It can also cause headaches, skin itching, and sensitivity to light.

Figure 5.3 Chinese sweet wormwood, shown here, has been used effectively in China and Thailand to reduce the symptoms of malaria. This herbal treatment is available in Europe but has not been approved for malarial treatment in the United States. (Photo by Scott Bauer, Courtesy Agricultural Research Service (ARS), U.S. Department of Agriculture)

It is isolated from the leaves of the sweet wormwood plant *Artemisia annua* (Figure 5.3), and it appears to be toxic to *Plasmodium.*

Artemisinin has been used medically in China for centuries. It was recently tested for effectiveness against *falciparum* malaria in Thailand, where malaria was becoming resistant to mefloquine, a historically effective drug. When artemisinin and mefloquine were given together to patients, the cure rate was 100 percent. Furthermore, since artemisinin has been used, mefloquine has increased in effectiveness. There have been several cases where artemisinin used in combination with standard drug therapies, such as quinine, has been shown to be very effective in treating malaria.

Artemisinin is available in China and Europe. It has not yet been approved for use in the United States. It has been shown to be safe and effective in Asia and its use is endorsed by the Wolrd Health Organization (WHO) for treatment of malaria in areas where the disease has become resistant to other treatments.

Numerous other traditional and herbal treatments exist for malaria. It has been estimated that more than 1,200 such treatments exist, and many of the plants that are used are becoming scarce. Some of the treatments reportedly provide excellent results, clearing the bloodstream of malaria parasites completely. Others may simply relieve the fevers associated with malaria and provide only relief. In some cases it is difficult to tell how effective the treatment is, because in areas where malaria is common, many of the people living there will have acquired some immunity. Still, it is reasonable to assume that any traditional treatment that has long been a part of the culture in which it is used will have at least some efficacy, and investigation of traditional and herbal treatments may well be worthwhile.[2]

Even with medicines for treatment available, malaria can still be extremely debilitating. In extreme cases, patients with *falciparum* malaria have to be hospitalized and, in some cases, given antibiotics and fluids intravenously. In serious cases, patients must have blood transfusions, kidney dialysis, and breathing assistance.

6

Attempts at Malarial Control

Malaria had been a problem in the southern United States during much of the first half of the twentieth century; some public health and government experts attribute the region's poverty and lack of industrial development to the disease. In South Carolina during the 1930s, it accounted for 16 out of every 100,000 deaths, and it was at its worst in the rural counties. The construction of the Santee-Cooper Reservoir System promised to make the situation worse by providing more breeding grounds for mosquitoes. Much of the credit for preventing a potential catastrophe belongs to Philip Gadsden Hasell, a sanitary engineer with the South Carolina Public Service Authority, who supervised the crews working on malaria control. Under his supervision, the crews cleared vegetation on which mosquitoes could rest, applied oil to standing water in which they could breed, dug ditches and installed drainage tile to drain standing water where practical, and applied screens to houses. On his watch Works Progress Administration (WPA) workers received typhoid inoculations, and the civilian population was tested for malaria. In 1943, Hasell began malaria control work for the U.S. Army.

Since the attack on the World Trade Center on September 11, 2001, the vulnerability of the United States to terrorists has become a reality to millions of people. Although most people do not worry about hijacked airplanes being flown into their houses, many do worry about **bioterrorism**. The thought of receiving an anthrax-laden letter had many people petrified for months. Indeed, letters contaminated with anthrax were sent to a newspaper and television studios. Some postal workers who handled such letters developed the disease, and a few of them died. There was a lot of talk about anthrax as a weapon, as there was about smallpox and perhaps botulism. There was also an attempt to release a culture of disease organisms into a Tokyo subway by a cult group in Japan, and a possible terrorist cell was discovered in England in the process of manufacturing ricin, a deadly poison isolated from the castor bean plant.

No one seems to be trying to use malaria as a **bioweapon.** Unlike the diseases that are most feared in biological warfare, malaria cannot be grown easily in culture. Malaria requires living hosts in which to grow, and those hosts must be human. Malaria that affects humans cannot be grown in laboratory animals. Secondly, because there is no way malaria could be spread from person to person by either direct contact or by contaminated media, the logistics of distributing the disease throughout a susceptible population render it impossible. Malaria requires a specific mosquito vector and raising and releasing a large number of malaria-laiden mosquitoes is impractical. Consequently, despite the devastation malaria has caused on humans throughout history, it cannot be used as a weapon.

Characteristics that render malaria ineffective as a weapon, such as the fact that it is not contagious, are also points of vulnerability that can be exploited in dealing with the disease. Infected patients can be treated with medication to cure them, as is the case with most other infections. Additionally, because malaria is completely dependent upon the *Anopheles* mosquito as a vector, and because the life cycle of that vector is well known and understood, it can be disrupted to prevent transfer of the disease among susceptible people. In short, to eliminate malaria, one might declare war on the mosquitoes that spread it.

THE WAR AGAINST MOSQUITOES
Similarly to the endemic malarial conditions of the southern United States in the early twentieth century, a region of Italy

around Rome known as the Campagna had festered with malaria since the days of the Roman Empire. In both cases, the disease was eliminated and both regions, after which these regions enjoyed greater prosperity than they had previously. To a large extent, the malaria was controlled by going after the vector of the disease, the *Anopheles* mosquito.

To fight a war effectively, one must know one's enemy. In the case of the *Anopheles* mosquito, scientists know a lot. In fact, once the relationship between the mosquito and the *Plasmodium* parasites became understood, it became evident that eliminating the mosquito alternative host and vector would eliminate the disease.

The *Anopheles* mosquito has a two-part life cycle: an aquatic larval and pupal stage and a terrestrial adult stage, during which it spreads malaria. During its larval stage, the *Anopheles* mosquito is strongly tied to the surface of the water in which it lives, more so, in fact, than other genera of mosquitoes. That is perhaps the most vulnerable part of the mosquito's life, and it was how the war against them was initially fought. In most areas where this was done successfully, malaria was brought under control.

DESTROYING THE ENEMY'S HOMELAND

Mosquitoes require standing water to reproduce. Therefore, eliminating standing water is a major step in controlling them. This action turned out to be part of several successful highly integrated attempts to deal with malaria.

In Italy, malaria was brought under control, in part, during the dictatorship of Benito Mussolini, between World Wars I and II. Mussolini instituted a program to drain the swamps in which the mosquitoes were breeding. In Havana, Cuba, around 1900, William C. Gorgas, a United States Army physician who had previously helped bring malaria and yellow fever under control in the Panama canal, practically eliminated malaria by larval control, including drainage of breeding sites. In the southern United States, two major projects contributed to bringing malaria under control. The first was the drainage of swamps and clearing land for agriculture and other uses by the WPA, a New Deal agency of the Roosevelt administration that was formed to put people to work. While malaria control may not have been the intention of the WPA, it was a clear result. The second was the formation of the Tennessee Valley Authority and the subsequent damming and channelization of the Tennessee River system for navigation, flood control, and power generation.[1]

Ironically, in the Tennessee River watershed, despite the fact that most freely flowing rivers were channelized and dammed to form large reservoirs for navigation and power generation, malaria did not spread. The common *Anopheles* mosquito in the region, *Anopheles quadrimaculatus*, breeds along the margins of large bodies of water. It would seem that the reservoirs should have provided a perfect location for breeding. However, the practice of letting water out of the reservoirs to maintain flow in the rivers left mosquito larvae stranded in small puddles, where they died as the puddles dried. Moreover, riverbanks were kept free of debris; mosquitoes that did emerge had no place to rest.

THE SECOND FRONT—CHEMICAL WARFARE

Physical elimination of mosquito breeding grounds, although effective, was not always practical. Cities did not want the ponds in their parks drained, for example. Consequently, a second front in the war was necessary. The front came in the form of the insecticide "Paris green."

Paris green (cupric acetoarsenite, $C_4H_6As_6Cu_4O_{16}$), is an organic, copper salt of the element arsenic, a known poison. It was first used in 1867 to control the Colorado potato beetle. In 1920, it was dispersed by airplanes in the swamps of Louisiana against mosquitoes. In many respects, Paris green is ideal for dealing with mosquito larvae, particularly *Anopheles* larvae.

Paris green is not soluble in water. It has to be dissolved in kerosene to be sprayed. The solution floats on the surface where *Anopheles* larvae feed. Consequently, the larvae are exposed to the poison, but the animals that live within the water are not. In particular, the small amounts that are effective against the

INSECTICIDES

Insecticides, by definition, are poisons that are used specifically to kill insects, just as fungicides are used on fungal pests and herbicides are used on weeds. Paris green and DDT are only two of thousands of different chemicals used to kill insect pests. Many insecticides are natural, or organic, in the popular sense. For example, pyrethrum, which is isolated from chrysanthemums, is an effective insecticide. Rotenone is isolated from the roots of a certain tropical tree. Natural insecticides are often biodegradable, which means they are naturally broken down by microorganisms and must be reapplied frequently. Even nicotine, a natural product of tobacco leaves that has been associated with the harmful effects of smoking, has been used as a natural insecticide. Synthetic pesticides, in contrast, are often persistent—they remain effective for weeks or months after they are applied.

DDT is part of a family of synthetic insecticides called the chlorinated hydrocarbons, which also includes chlordane and toxaphene. These are particularly persistent chemicals—that is, they do not degrade in nature, and their residues can accumulate in animal tissues. The other major family of synthetics is the organophosphates, which include Malathion and Parathion. These are also effective insecticides; but, unlike the chloronated hydrocarbons, they do readily degrade. For example, more than 50 percent of the Malathion that is applied to a field of sandy soil may break down overnight. Consequently, organophosphates must be applied more frequently.

mosquito larvae appear to have no impact on fish and wildlife, including fish that eat mosquito larvae. However, it is difficult to believe that the kerosene in which Paris green is dissolved is harmless and a common result of spraying Paris green was oily messes washing up on lake shores.

Paris green was used in the United States in standing water that could not be drained. It contributed significantly to the elimination of malaria. It was effective elsewhere as well, for example in Egypt and Brazil, where *falciparum* malaria was causing problems. Paris green was also part of Mussolini's war against mosquitoes in Italy. After World War II, Paris green was replaced by other compounds, including one that chemists of the time believed to be a chemical miracle: DDT.

DDT ($C_{14}H_9Cl_5$) or dichloro-diphenyl-trichloroethane, is a member of the family of organic chemicals known as the chlorinated hydrocarbons (Figure 6.1). It was invented by Othmar Zieller, a German pharmacist, in 1874. Paul Hermann Müller, a Swiss chemist, experimentally exposed mosquitoes to DDT. In 1939, he showed how effective it was against insects. In 1948, Müller was awarded a Nobel Prize for his discovery.

At first DDT was very effective in killing insects, including mosquitoes and other disease vectors. It appeared to be harmless to people if only because it is not readily absorbed through the skin.[2] It was first used during World War II when it was sprayed in the South Pacific to control malaria. Given the problem that malaria presented to American troops, one can only imagine what the war would have been like had the chemical not been used. DDT was also used in Europe to kill typhus-carrying lice. After the war, it was used extensively in agriculture to combat plant pests as well as in disease control. In India, it reduced malaria incidence from 75 million cases to fewer than 5 million during a 10-year period. DDT did not just kill insects on contact, it also remained active in soil or on plants, killing weeks, even months, after it was applied.

DDT (Dichloro-diphenyl-trichloroethane)

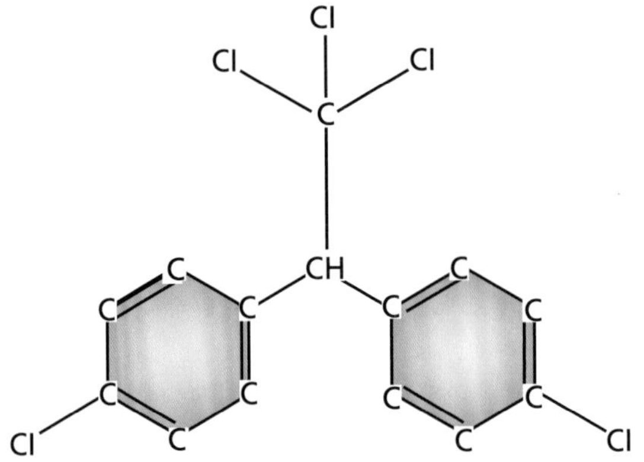

© Infobase Publishing

Figure 6.1 DDT (Dichloro-diphenyl-trichloroethane), shown as a molecule here, was a very popular insecticide that was first used to kill mosquitoes during World War II. Although effective in the short term, this chemical remains active in the soil and in animals' bodies, allowing it to be transferred up the food chain in ever-increasing concentrations. This is called bioaccumulation.

DDT may have been too effective. In many cases, it was abused. By the late 1940s, DDT was sprayed regularly on trees (Figure 6.2) to kill not only mosquitoes, but also tree pests and other irritating insects. There was no danger from malaria, yellow fever, or any other insect-borne disease: It was sprayed to make life more comfortable. DDT was packaged in aerosol cans to kill houseflies. It was used liberally on farms to kill animal pests.

In the 1950s, problems with DDT began to accumulate. Because it did not readily degrade into harmless substances in the environment. When it did degrade, it was only slightly, and its breakdown products were toxic, too. Consequently, DDT could migrate from its point of application out to forests and waterways. Here, it entered the natural food chain and accumulated in the tissues of animals and even people.

Second, DDT is a nonselective poison. It kills not only its target insects, but others as well. DDT killed beneficial insects such as bees, butterflies, and other pollinating and predatory insects such as dragonflies and praying mantises that ate insect pests. It also killed insects and other small animals such as worms upon which birds fed. Thirdly, its effectiveness against pests began to wane as the more susceptible members of insect pest species were eliminated and more resistant ones survived. It got to the point in some places that the only way to kill a mosquito with DDT was to hit it with the can.

The old expression, "Anything that seems too good to be true probably is," can be applied to DDT. Even Paul Hermann Müller worried about the future effects of DDT. In 1962, marine biologist Rachel Carson published *Silent Spring*, a book in which she documented the growing environmental threat that DDT was presenting. Carson has often been credited as the individual around whom the environmental movement of the 1960s began, although many, especially those within the agrochemical industry, disputed her arguments at the time. In reality, there were a number of important contributors to the environmental movement. However, Carson's book encouraged people to question the safety and effectiveness of DDT.

Research on the threats of DDT supported many of the claims made against the pesticide. By 1973, DDT spraying in the United States was banned. The decision did not sit well with everyone. The petrochemical industry that produced DDT was not pleased that a profitable product had been outlawed, farmers were concerned that their productivity would decline, and public health officials worried about epidemics of vector-borne diseases reoccurring.

The last concern was not an empty worry. Indeed, there has been an increase in the frequency of malaria in parts of the world, particularly Africa, in recent years, and many health authorities would like to see DDT reintroduced. However, it is questionable that the ban on DDT is responsible for the resurgence of malaria or any other vector-borne disease. Many countries outside of the United States, including several that export produce to the United States, continue to use DDT. Many countries where malaria occurs also use DDT. It is likely that the recent increases in malaria cases there are more due to the resistance of mosquitoes to DDT and the resistance of *Plasmodium* protozoa to antimalarial medications than to the DDT ban.

Figure 6.2   Spraying trees with DDT was a popular way to control insect populations in the 1950s. While this killed mosquitoes, it also killed insects that were beneficial to humans; DDT also built up in the soil and in animals' bodies, which had a devastating impact on wildlife. Here, workers are spraying trees in Connecticut after a flood in 1955. (Courtesy CDC/Public Health Image Library)

DDT RESISTANCE

The same mechanism that causes drug resistance in malaria protozoa applies to mosquitoes and DDT. Some mosquitoes are naturally resistant to the poison. For reasons that are not understood, some mosquitoes have experienced gene mutations that allow them to decompose DDT. Gene mutations can also increase the resistance of a population of mosquitoes over time, especially as DDT selectively eliminates the more susceptible members. This resistance has already occurred.

THE THIRD FRONT–PHYSICAL WARFARE

Destroying mosquito breeding grounds and poisoning insects accomplished much in terms of controlling malaria, but other methods were applied as well. In rural areas, for example, water that accumulated in abandoned tires became mosquito breeding grounds. Proper disposal of the tires, and anything else in which water could collect, reduced mosquitoes' opportunities to breed. In addition, putting screens on windows prevented mosquitoes from biting people. Screening windows did not reduce the number of mosquitoes, but it probably forced mosquitoes to find other victims, animals in particular, in which the *Plasmodium* protozoan could not survive. Malaria was wiped out in the United States because of the combination of actions used against them: drainage, pesticides, and window screens. Treatment with medications, as described in the previous chapter, also contributed significantly to eliminating malaria. Although mosquitoes managed to survive, reproduce, find victims, and become resistant to pesticides, the absence of disease reservoirs meant that malaria could not be spread.

IN CONCLUSION

The war against mosquitoes will never be won. The insects are too plastic genetically to remain vulnerable to pesticides and

(continues on page 72)

BIOACCUMULATION

In addition to being synthetic, DDT is fat soluble. If a mosquito absorbs some DDT, but too little to kill it, the animal's body cannot break down the chemical. Instead, the DDT is absorbed into the animal's fat, where it remains. A dragonfly that eats the mosquito would then acquire the DDT from the mosquito. The dragonfly would be unable to break down the DDT, which would be stored in its fat, as would any DDT in all of the mosquitoes the dragonfly ate. If a fish eats the dragonfly, the DDT gets stored in the fish's fat, as does the DDT in all of the bugs and smaller animals the fish eats. In this way, DDT gets concentrated in fatty tissue as it is passed through a food chain, a string of one animal eating another. By the time an osprey eats the fish, it is getting a pretty concentrated dose of DDT. If the osprey eats enough contaminated fish, it may accumulate enough DDT to cause internal harm. This buildup of DDT is called bioaccumulation.

DDT causes substantial damage in the reproductive systems of birds. It disrupts the series of reactions that put calcium into the shells of the eggs that birds produce. Thus, birds that have been exposed to high amounts of DDT may produce eggs with very thin shells (Figure 6.3), which easily break, or eggs with no shells at all. Baby birds cannot develop in such eggs and die.

DDT can accumulate in people as well. Farm workers who are exposed to the chemical may end up with it in their tissues, as can people who eat a lot of contaminated fish. In people, DDT often ends up in the liver and in fatty tissue, including the mammary tissue of women's breasts. In women who are lactating (producing milk), DDT can be passed on to their babies when they nurse.

There is no conclusive evidence that DDT is harmful to people. But DDT has been shown to cause cancer in laboratory animals; therefore, it is potentially carcinogenic for humans as well. Furthermore, because DDT kills some animals and interrupts the reproductive systems of others, it could possibly harm people as well.

Other harmful environmental contaminants called polychlorinated biphenyls (PCBs) are chemically similar to DDT. The two chemicals can be confused during testing. Consequently, it is sometimes difficult to know which one, if not both, may be present. PCBs cause identifiable problems in animals that receive a large enough dose. Scientists are fairly certain that PCBs can harm humans.

Figure 6.3 In birds, DDT bioaccumulation caused weakened or broken eggshells, in which baby birds cannot survive. Examples of such eggs are shown here. (© Galen Rowell/CORBIS)

(continued from page 69)
too opportunistic not to take advantage of breeding opportunities we present them. But attempts at combinations of strategies may help in returning them to being an annoyance rather than a disease vector.

Nobody really knows why malaria was eliminated in the United States. Between 1947 and 1951, a cooperative effort in 13 states in the South known as the United States Malaria Eradication Program worked to get DDT applied to rural homes in counties where malaria had been reported. That, the drainage of breeding areas, and the installation of window screens all contributed to the success of the program. There was concern on the part of health agencies that American soldiers returning at the ends of World War II, the Korean conflict, and the Vietnam conflict would bring malaria back with them, touch off new epidemics, and reestablish malaria in the United States, particularly in the South. It never happened, and again, nobody really knows why. However, much work was carried on by the U.S. Public Health Service, and it probably deserves as much of the credit as anyone.

Elsewhere in the world, attempts at malaria control were less successful. Malaria was eliminated from Western Europe, but it remained a problem in the tropics. Historically, attempts were made at controlling malaria by avoiding it. During the colonial period in Africa, European administrators tended to live in so-called malaria-free zones, areas that were not mosquito prone, while African natives were not afforded the same luxury. In 1955, the WHO attempted a global elimination of malaria in a program similar to the United States Malaria Eradication Program. Although successful in Europe and Australia, it was less so in Asia and South America, and it never got off the ground in Africa.

Today, attempts at mosquito control continue. For example, in Sichuan Province in China, the draining of rice paddies when not in use rather than letting them sit full of water year round has contributed to the reduction of malaria there.[3] Similar activities have been employed elsewhere. In Africa, various methods have been combined, including the use of bed nets impregnated with insecticide. Overuse of DDT led to the evolution of resistant mosquitoes; these other methods of mosquito control may hold promise.

7
Preventing Malaria

Among the drawbacks to using pesticides against mosquitoes is collateral damage, the destruction of non-target organisms. A promising exception to this generalization is a toxin isolated from the bacterium *Bacillus thuringiensis,* a relative of anthrax. Known as BT, *Bacillus thuringiensis* toxin is harmless to most organisms but deadly to many species of flies, including mosquitoes. In the Peruvian Amazon, where malaria is a problem, researchers from the Instituto de Medicina Tropical Alexander von Humboldt in Lima have developed an ingenious way of producing the toxin in nature. The procedure involves growing BT in a "tea" made by boiling yucca plants. The tea, a potent mosquito larvicide, is then poured into ponds where mosquitoes breed. Thus, by killing the mosquito larvae, the vector's life cycle is disrupted and malaria is prevented.

AVOIDING THE BITE

To get malaria, a person must be bitten by a malaria-infected mosquito. The best way to avoid getting bitten by a mosquito is to avoid mosquitoes entirely. Doing that requires knowledge of the mosquito's behavior and adjusting one's own behavior to compensate. For example, mosquitoes are most active at dusk and dawn, so avoiding outdoor activity at those times limits exposure to the insect. Additionally, mosquitoes are able to "see" heat. Sense organs on their antennae detect infrared light, which our bodies radiate when we shed heat. Wearing protective clothing, particularly light-colored clothing that radiates infrared light much less than darker clothes, helps to avoid a mosquito's bite.

ELIMINATING BREEDING GROUNDS

Other means of avoiding mosquitoes involve limiting their opportunities to breed and find you when you are vulnerable. In the previous chapter, it was mentioned that abandoned tires collect rainwater and provide ideal locations where mosquitoes can breed. Mosquitoes can also breed in swimming pools, birdbaths, fountains, animal watering troughs, roof gutters, and even in carelessly discarded cans and beverage containers. Denying mosquitoes access to such objects, by keeping them dry whenever possible, or removing litter where water can accumulate, limits the opportunities of mosquitoes to reproduce. In cases where water must stand, as in swimming pools, chemicals such as chlorine can be added to the water to kill mosquito larvae. In some cases, mosquito fish (*Gambusia affinis*) can be introduced into water. These are small fish that eat mosquito larvae.

USING PROTECTIVE BARRIERS

Protective barriers are anything that physically blocks a mosquito's access to its prey. Window screening represents a coarse barrier. Theoretically, it should prevent mosquitoes from entering a house, and it certainly reduces the number that gain access, but it is less than perfect. Screens can become damaged. Many houses are leaky, particularly in poor countries and even in the poor sections of wealthy ones. Consequently, mosquitoes often find their way around window screens, and everyone has experienced the annoying whine of a mosquito around his or her ears while lying in bed at night and has woken up in the morning with a bite, despite the screens in the windows. However, by reducing the number of mosquitoes that enter a house, window screens do reduce the risk of malaria to the people inside it.

Another protective barrier that can work quite effectively is bed netting. Bed netting can be even more effective when impregnated with insect repellents or, better still, insecticide. This procedure is being used now in Africa. In Ethiopia, in particular, the Carter Center, an organization founded by former United States President Jimmy Carter and his wife

MOSQUITO FISH

Mosquito fish (*Gambusia affinis*) are semitropical fish that were originally native to the southeastern United States, Central America, and the Caribbean. Unlike most fish these are live-bearing fish, which means that they give birth to living young rather than laying eggs that hatch later. They are similar to and related to the guppy. In nature, mosquito fish grow larger than the guppy. Males reach a length of one to two inches, but females can grow up to twice that length. Mosquito fish prefer quiet waters more than rapidly flowing streams and rivers. The fish will feed voraciously, not exclusively on mosquito larvae, but also on other small aquatic animals, including other fish and their own offspring. Because of their affinity for mosquito larvae, mosquito fish have been transplanted across much of the world, particularly into areas where malaria is a problem. Mosquito fish are able to function under conditions of low oxygen, making them effective even in stagnant water where mosquitoes can breed but their predators often cannot survive.

Unfortunately, there are disadvantages to introducing mosquito fish to areas where they are not native. Mosquito fish tend to eat the larvae of other fishes, as well as tadpoles of tree frogs and aquatic insects, in addition to mosquito larvae. Mosquito fish are best used to control mosquito populations in isolated ponds and ditches and backyard water-holding structures such as garden ponds. In water bodies with other animals, other mosquito larvae-eating fish such as fathead minnows may be a better choice.

Rosalynn, in partnership with Emory University, has been providing people with bed netting impregnated with pyrethrum, a natural insecticide extracted from chrysanthemums. Elsewhere in Africa, bed netting impregnated with the synthetic pesticide permethrin is being used and in limited studies has been shown to be effective in reducing both the incidence of and number of deaths from malaria. Although bed nets are one of the least expensive interventions, there is some question about whether the practice is being implemented everywhere it could be.

USING REPELLENTS

Sometimes, however, mosquitoes simply cannot be avoided. Certain areas such as deep woods or swamps have mosquito populations that may be so dense and/or hungry that the mosquitos may be active at all hours, including in bright sunlight. Moreover, there are times when people have to be out at dusk or dawn. In such cases, chemical mosquito repellents can be used to prevent bites.

Everybody has had the experience of coming across a smell that is so putrid that he or she wants to get far away from it as quickly as possible. Ideally, that is what a good insect repellent does to mosquitoes. The repellent makes the person wearing it seem too unappealing to bite. Alternatively, a repellent could block a mosquito's receptors for finding victims. Additionally, a good repellent must be harmless to people, must not be washed away by perspiration or water, and must be long lasting so that it does not have to be reapplied frequently.

One material that is popularly used as a mosquito repellent is Skin-So-Soft®, a bath oil that is marketed by Avon Products, Inc. Although it is not intended to be a mosquito repellent, it does seem to work as one, probably because its odor is offensive to mosquitoes. In one respect, it is ideal: It is not harmful. However, this product apparently evaporates from the skin and does not protect for very long. Permethrin (a potent insecticide), in

Figure 7.1 Using protective barriers, such as screens and mosquito nets, can help guard against mosquito bites. Often, mosquito nets are coated in mosquito repellents and hung over beds. This woman is washing her mosquito net in a chemical repellent solution. (© Nic Bothma/EPA/CORBIS)

contrast, is effective for a long time, but is too toxic to be applied directly to skin or to clothing. However, it can be impregnated into bed nets. The most effective mosquito repellents are those that contain the compound known as DEET.

Known chemically as N,N-diethyl-meta-toluamide, DEET ($C_{12}H_{17}NO$) is perhaps the most effective commercially available mosquito repellent available today. Accepted by the U.S. Environmental Protection Agency, it is long lasting and generally not harmful if used properly. It should not be used in concentrations of more than 50 percent for adults and 10 percent for children under two years of age. It can cause allergic problems in infants and young children. The safest and most effective concentration is between 15 and 30 percent. DEET can be applied to skin or to clothing. Excessive amounts can cause skin irritation, rashes, and, in excessive doses, nerve damage. It can also cause irritation to the cornea if it gets in the eye. It can irritate the mucus membranes of the mouth or nose if it comes into contact with them. Exactly how DEET works to repel mosquitoes is not known. It has been reported to block the nervous receptors the mosquito uses to locate prey.

DEET is present in most commercially familiar insect repellents, such as Off® or Cutter®. It is not harmful if it is used only on skin, not moist tissues, and it is not used in large concentrations. Moreover, DEET is long lasting. A single application of a DEET-containing repellent can keep mosquitoes away for several hours.

Other mosquito repellents exist. Citronella oil, for example, is a plant derivative that has repellent properties. It is available in topical sprays, but it is less effective than DEET. Citronella candles have long been used by campers and backyard picnickers. They protect people close by but not farther away, and they are no more effective than ordinary candles. It may be that the heat and carbon dioxide emitted by candles act as decoys, thus luring the mosquitoes away from human victims.[1]

Figure 7.2 Mosquito nets have greatly reduced the incidences of malaria, particularly in Africa. Sleeping under a mosquito net protects people from being bitten by mosquitoes while they sleep. (© Henk Badenhorst/iStockphoto)

Pyrethrum, an extract from chrysanthemums and described earlier as an insecticide used to impregnate bed netting, also works as a repellent. It is effective and long lasting, and it can be impregnated into textile fabrics that are made into clothing.[2]

Two other chemicals are endorsed by the Centers for Disease Control as repellents: picaridin, a synthetic; and oil of lemon and eucalyptus, an extract of plants. Picaridin ($C_{12}H_{23}F_9NO_3$), developed by Bayer AG, is also known as KBR3023 or by the Bayer AG trademark Bayrepel. It is reportedly as effective as DEET with lower toxicity. It is available in a repellent offered by Cutter®. Oil of lemon and eucalyptus is also available commercially in their repellent Repel®.

Finally, wormwood (*Artemisia* spp.), an ornamental plant, produces an oil that upon extraction can be used as a repellent. It is now being used in Africa to impregnate bed netting.

There are some traditional means of repelling mosquitoes that have questionable effectiveness. For example, 25 to 50 mg per day of vitamin B_1 (thiamine) supposedly repels mosquitoes. When supplied in excess, the body uses whatever it needs and excretes the remainder through the skin pores with perspiration. It takes about two weeks for skin levels to get high enough to be repulsive to mosquitoes. Consequently, one would have to start taking the vitamin well before a planned outing. Some people claim that using this has kept mosquitoes away from them; others claim it does nothing. Vitamin B_1 excess is not known to be harmful, but taking too much of any substance is not recommended without a doctor's advice. Similarly, garlic is said to repel mosquitoes if consumed in sufficient amounts. It too is excreted through the pores and garlic based sprays are commercially available. Although it may or may not work against mosquitoes, too much of it will keep people away as well.

Folk medicine has it that vitamin C is also offensive to mosquitoes, and vitamin C-based sprays are also available. Whether or not this is accurate, consuming vitamin C in large doses is not an effective way to repel mosquitoes. Any excess one consumes is eliminated through urine, not perspiration.

MALARIA PROPHYLAXIS

Medically speaking, the term *prophylaxis* means prevention. Thus getting a flu shot is an example of a prophylactic act. At the moment, a vaccine does not exist that will prevent malaria, but several medications that are used to treat malaria are also effective in preventing it. Malaria prophylaxis is usually given to somebody who is not normally exposed to malaria, but is going to be traveling in an area where malaria is present.

As mentioned, many of the medications that are used to treat malaria are also effective in preventing it. These drugs are

A CASE HISTORY: BURUNDI

Burundi is a small country in central Africa just south of the equator, west of Tanzania and north of Lake Tanganyika. It is a poor country, one that has been torn by political strife in the past and now suffers from a very high incidence of AIDS. As with much of tropical Africa, Burundi also suffers from a high incidence of *falciparum* malaria. In the autumn of 2000, Burundi was experiencing 300 deaths per month. Moreover, the malaria parasites in Burundi have become highly resistant to chloroquine and a combination of sulfadoxine and pyrimethamine, the usual drugs of choice for treating malaria in Africa. Since 2000, with the financial support of the European Commission's Humanitarian Aid Office, the World Health Organization, and UNICEF, Burundi has adopted a promising way to treat malaria. The treatment involves a rapid treatment of malaria (i.e., within 24 hours of symptom onset), and uses a combination of artesunate and amodiaquine. This treatment regimen is reported to be more than 95 percent effective. In addition, the organization Roll Back Malaria is working to provide pesticide-impregnated bed nets and indoor residual house spraying to control mosquitoes and thus prevent malaria.

usually given to somebody who will be traveling into an area where malaria is a risk. The patient starts taking the medication before he or she begins the trip and continues for a period of time after he or she returns. The exact regimen depends on the specific drug prescribed.

In the case of chloroquine, where it is still effective, the patient begins taking the drug one week before the trip and continues for four weeks afterward, usually taking one pill each week. The same is true for mefloquine. Doxycycline is taken daily. It can be started one or two days before travel and can be continued for four weeks after return. Malarone® is also taken beginning two days before travel. It is taken daily and continued for one week once the trip is over.

Malaria medications can cause some undesirable side effects, including stomach upset and severe vomiting. Over an extended period of time, these side effects could cause dehydration.

Modern prophylaxis against many diseases involves vaccination, essentially tricking the body into developing an immunity without putting it at risk of having the disease. Work on a malaria vaccine has been ongoing since the early twentieth century without much success. There are a number of obstacles to developing a malaria vaccine. For the moment, suffice it to say that in spite of those obstacles, recent breakthroughs in research have occurred, and a vaccine is in development.[3]

ROLL BACK MALARIA

Because malaria is a global problem, the best solution is also likely to be global. "Roll Back Malaria" (RBM), a global partnership jointly founded by the World Health Organization, the United Nations Development Programme, UNICEF, and the World Bank in 1998, was started in Africa, where malaria is at its worst. The program includes national governments, research institutions, private organizations, professional societies, United Nations and developmental agencies, and the media.

The goal of the program is to reduce the frequency of malaria by half by the year 2010. It addresses the problem of malaria in several ways, including prevention and treatment. Prevention involves using pesticide-impregnated bed nets.

The treatment involves medications using intelligence-based interventions, which means using geographic information systems to apply drugs and insecticides only where they are effective and needed. If, for example, the *Plasmodium* in a particular region of Africa is resistant to chloroquine, it would be senseless to use chloroquine; some other medication would have to be used. The drug treatment is given in a clinical setting, using whatever drug or drug combination is effective in that area. The program also wants to expand the use of effective treatments and to respond rapidly whenever an outbreak occurs. A particularly important target for both prevention and treatment is pregnant women, because malaria can fatally harm both the mother and her unborn child. The program does not call for widespread spraying of pesticides to kill mosquitoes, because that has been shown to be ineffective in the long term.

A third part of the program is the support of research for better treatments. This endeavor includes a subprogram called Medicines for Malaria Venture (MMV), which works to raise money for the support of new drug development. The program's initial target was to raise $15 million by 2001. The group eventually wants to raise $30 million per year. A long-term goal is to become self-supporting by selling drugs that were developed with program support. MMV hopes to accomplish this goal by 2010.

HUMANITARIAN ORGANIZATIONS AND FOUNDATIONS

In addition to Roll Back Malaria, numerous other charitable groups are working toward the control of malaria. The Carter Center is involved in malaria control in Ethiopia with the distribution of pesticide-impregnated bed nets in addition to supporting other interventions. Between 2004 and 2007, Ethiopia experienced a decline in malaria commensurate with the bed nets distributed. The Carter Center is also involved in work to prevent other problematic diseases in Africa, including river blindness and lymphatic filariasis (elephantiasis). Supported by grants and donations, this organization is helping in some of the most impoverished places around the world.[4]

Another participant in the war against malaria is the Bill and Melinda Gates Foundation. Like the Carter Center, this foundation supports many humanitarian efforts around the planet, and malaria is one into which it puts much effort. With substantial financial grants, it has been supporting malaria control by providing bed nets, facilitating targeted household spraying with pesticides, and developing of medications, including a vaccine.

Malaria No More is an organization that works at educating about malaria. It describes its mission as ending malaria deaths, and it functions in Africa. Working from donations, it also distributes bed nets in areas where malaria is endemic.

Finally, the Global Fund to Fight AIDS, Tuberculosis, and Malaria is a funding agency that provides financial resources to combat the three infections in its name. It is worldwide in activity, and it supports the coordination of multiple activities to promote human health.

8

Malaria Now

The threat of malaria being imported into the United States in an ill immigrant is illustrated by the case of a three-year-old Tanzanian girl, who was diagnosed with *falciparum* malaria in her native country in May 2007. She was successfully treated with quinine, though of unknown exact formulation and dose, and she was given a subsequent treatment with sulfadoxine-pyrimethamine during an examination prior to her departure for the United States, a requirement to enter the country. A month later she was admitted to a children's hospital, where a blood exam revealed the presence of *P. falciparum*. She was successfully treated with orally atovaquone-proguanil and, after five days, was released from the hospital.

If Sir Alexander Fleming, the British scientist who discovered penicillin, were alive today, he would probably be astonished to find out that his discovery was now ineffective in combating many of the disease germs that it easily wiped out at the time of his death. Likewise, if William C. Gorgas, the U.S. Army physician who helped in the control of malaria and yellow fever in Panama and nearly wiped out malaria in Cuba, were to return today, he would most likely also be astonished to learn that the disease has not been brought under control worldwide. The reality is, however, that over most of the world, malaria is as much of a problem now as it was 50 years ago, or perhaps even worse (Figure 8.1). Today, populations of mosquitoes are resistant to DDT, and there are varieties of *Plasmodium* that are resistant to antimalarial medications.

There have been some successes in the war against malaria. The disease is no longer a problem in North America, Europe, much (but not all) of Central America, and many islands in the South Pacific. It is also not nearly the problem in South America that it once was. Otherwise,

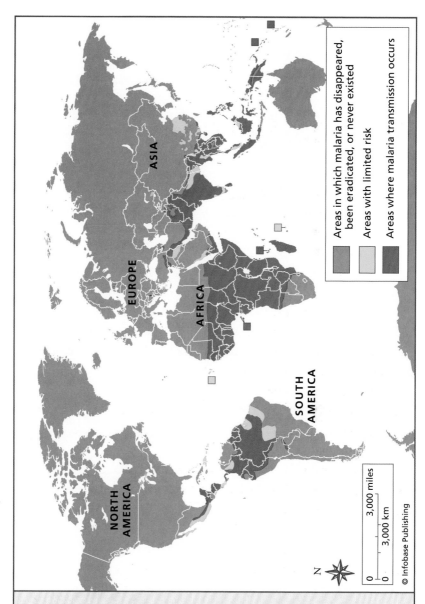

Figure 8.1 Malaria is most prevalent in northern South America, Africa, and India. However, malaria can become a worldwide problem if the *Plasmodium* parasite is carried to an uninfected area of the world, either in a mosquito or in a human, and spread among other mosquitoes in that area.

however, malaria is present over much of the world. In fact, malaria, tuberculosis (a bacterial infection of the lungs), and schistosomiasis (a disease caused by a parasitic worm), in combination, kill more people worldwide than any other combination of three diseases (Talbe 8.1). Of the three, only tuberculosis appears to be a current threat in the United States. Schistosomiasis most probably will never occur in the United States because to complete its life cycle it requires a species of snail that cannot live there. The islands of Hawaii and Puerto Rico are exceptions. Malaria has occurred in the United States in the past, and it could return.

IN AFRICA

Although some of the worst malarial drug resistance is in Asia, most cases of malaria are occurring in Africa. About 80 percent of the world's malaria exists there. As in the past, its persistence is facilitated by the behavior of the people who live there. In the African countries of Ethiopia and Namibia, for example, people

Table 8.1   The Leading Infectious Causes of Death in Low-Income Countries, 2002

Lower respiratory infections	2.86 million
HIV/AIDS	2.14 million
Diarrheal diseases	1.54 million
Malaria	1.24 million
Tuberculosis	1.10 million

As of 2002, malaria was one of the leading causes of death by an infectious disease in poor countries. Lower respiratory diseases were the leading cause of death, with malaria appearing fourth. It caused 1.24 million deaths in 2002, up by 140,000 from 2000.

Source: World Health Organization Fact Sheet 310. March 2007.

use soil to make mud bricks, which they use in constructing their homes. The activity leaves pits in the soil that can fill with water in which the common mosquito of the region, Anopheles gambiae, breeds. Anopheles gambiae is somewhat unique in that it can take advantage of these small, water-flled depresssions. Most species of Anopheles do better in larger bodies of water. Because the people of the region are farmers that grow corn, mosquito larvae feed on corn pollen that lands on the water. Once they become adults, the mosquitoes are able to travel a distance of about two miles, about 3.2 kilometers, from their breeding sites. People living within that area become the mosquitoes' victims.

It may seem that the situation could easily be controlled if the Namibian and Ethiopian people could be persuaded to find other means of building their homes. However, the behavior pattern is perhaps culturally engrained, and changing such a pattern is not easy. In addition, there are precious few resources in the region. Mud bricks are sometimes the only material available for home construction. Moreover, there is a lot of poverty and rapid population growth in both countries, two factors that complicate matters. If other materials were available for home construction, most of the people might not be able to afford them.

A POTENTIAL WORLDWIDE THREAT

Although malaria mostly affects Asia and Africa at the moment, it can potentially erupt into a worldwide problem very quickly. There are several reasons why this could happen. First, Americans and Europeans travel to areas with malaria rather regularly. **Ecotourism**, the environmentally responsible travel to natural environments like rain forests, has become extremely popular and many people who indulge in it expose themselves to tropical diseases. About 30,000 Americans and Europeans become infected with malaria every year because of travel. If these people return home unaware of their infections and Anopheles

MALARIA AND GLOBAL WARMING

Global warming is the worldwide increase in average annual temperature. For the past 100 years or more, the world has been becoming a warmer place. It is believed by many, including many if not most scientists, that humans are the cause of global warming.

Carbon dioxide, the gas that is given off as a result of combustion, is the practical culprit in global warming. It acts something like a blanket in that it prevents heat from escaping from the Earth. Since the industrial revolution, the burning of fossil fuel has increased the amount of carbon dioxide in the atmosphere and, therefore, increased the global temperature. Glaciers are melting faster than they are growing, the polar ice caps are thinning, and many species of plants and animals that live in the temperate regions of the world are extending their ranges into what have historically been colder climates. Additionally, some island nations, such as the Maldives and Seychelles in the Indian Ocean, have expressed concern that global warming has increased the sea level and is threatening their shorelines. The exact cause of the increasing temperatures worldwide is still under debate. Theoretically, the increase in temperature should exacerbate the risk of malaria spreading around the world because malaria is largely a tropical disease and *falciparum* malaria is almost entirely tropical. In theory, as world temperatures increase, the range of malaria would become larger as the mosquito season in the north temperate zone gets longer.

To date, there is no evidence that global warming has affected the distribution of malaria, and scientists disagree on what will happen. In fact, the recent increases in malaria cases have been linked to population growth and poverty. However, if the climate continues to warm, it may contribute to the spread of malaria in the future.

mosquitoes are around, there is a real risk that malaria will be spread. Indeed, epidemics can be started this way.

In 2002, a couple of cases of malaria showed up in the Washington, D.C., area. These were probably people who had been traveling abroad. Because Washington, D.C., is densely populated and also a popular tourist destination, the potential for malaria to spread rapidly was present. Because people from Washington, D.C., travel all over the country and over the world, a malaria outbreak in Washington, D.C., could easily spread to other places.

According to the Centers for Disease Control and Prevention, the number of malaria cases in the United States has fluctuated between 220 and 3,180 between 1971 and 2000. In 2000, for example, 1,402 cases of malaria were reported, a decrease of 138 cases from 1999. Only four of those cases were known to be acquired in the United States and none by mosquito bite. Two of them were infants whose mothers had malaria and the other two were by intravenous administration of contaminated blood. The remaining cases, more than 99 percent, were acquired abroad. In general then, the risk of a malaria outbreak in the United States appears to be minimal, but the potential continues to exist.[1]

The ease of long-distance travel, along with the short incubation period of malaria, makes it possible for malaria to be spread rapidly. Complicating the problem is the reality that most European and American physicians do not deal with malaria on a regular basis. Many of them would not recognize the symptoms right away. Consequently, somebody who is seeking treatment for malaria in Europe or the United States could easily be misdiagnosed and treated for the wrong disease.

Also possible, although much less likely, is that an infected mosquito could fly into the open cargo bay of an airliner in, say, the Philippines, sit on a wall, and fly out the next day when the plane is being unloaded in Los Angeles. It has been suggested that West Nile virus made its way from the Middle East to New York this way. Indeed, malaria spread from Africa to South America by mosquitoes hitching rides on fast mail boats a century ago. Malaria would be more easily contained than West Nile, which infects birds as well as people, but malaria can be more serious.

Malaria could conceivably spread across the world once more. This time, however, it will be caused by *Plasmodium* that is resistant to antibiotics. It may be spread by mosquitoes that are resistant to DDT. Moreover, global warming, a growing environmental concern, has the potential to make the problem even worse.

9
The Future of Malaria

In 1898, English author Herbert George (H.G.) Wells published his science fiction novel *The War of the Worlds*. In his book, an invasion from Mars was ultimately thwarted by the Earth's bacteria. The Martians, a technologically advanced civilization, had long since eliminated all lower forms of life from their planet, including **pathogenic** bacteria and other parasites. With no challenges, the Martians' immune systems degenerated. Upon being exposed to bacteria during their invasion of Earth, their immune systems failed to protect them and they died. The story is probably better known from the 2005 motion picture with Tom Cruise or Orson Welles' radio broadcast in 1938. The latter was so realistic that tens of thousands of people actually believed that the Earth was being invaded by aliens.

The theory behind H.G. Wells' story was faulty, of course. Many of the microorganisms with which we share our planet are essential for our existence. Eliminating them would cause our own extinction. It is extremely likely that eliminating bacteria would also eliminate all other forms of life on any other planet where life exists, if there are any. Still, many believe that as technology advances, humans will gain more control over biology, perhaps to the point where diseases and the organisms that cause them may be eliminated.

Currently, malaria can be found in 107 countries, and 40 percent of the world population is at risk of getting the disease. Every 30 seconds an African child dies from it. If malaria could be eliminated, much human suffering would be relieved. This chapter will consider this possibility. It is important to remember that the future is always uncertain.

THE ROLE OF GENES

In 1990, the United States began its part in the Human Genome Project, an international venture to determine the location of each gene on every human chromosome. In 2003 the project was completed, ahead of schedule and under budget. Part of the goal of the project is to better understand diseases with genetic components and hopefully to conquer them.

In the process, however, scientists have learned about the nature of genes in general and the biochemical processes that govern life. Moreover, they have gathered extensive knowledge about the genes and heredity of other forms of life as well, because the technology that was learned in mapping the human genome was applied to other forms of life.

If, or perhaps more appropriately when, the genome of the malaria protozoa is determined, the development of fully effective vaccines against them will be much easier, as described below.

THE IMMUNE SYSTEM

Some of the proteins that are produced by cells result from the unique combination of genes that an individual inherits. Of those unique proteins, some end up on cell surfaces, where they biochemically identify the individual who carries them. They essentially identify him or her as "self." Thus, when a disease organism with its unique genes and unique cell surface proteins enters a human body, it is recognized as "non-self."

The identification proteins of a parasite are recognized as foreign or antigens (Figure 9.1). The host responds by trying to reject the parasites. The host can reject the antigens by producing antibodies (Figure 9.2), proteins that attempt to destroy the invader's antigens. Antibodies are produced by one set of white blood cells called **lymphocytes**. Alternatively, the body can directly attack the antigen with another set of lymphocytes.

The mechanism by which the body fights an infection is quite similar to the mechanism by which it tries to reject a transplanted organ. For example, a transplanted heart has the identification proteins of the donor individual. In an organ recipient, those proteins would be considered antigens and would trigger an **immune response**. This process is called tissue rejection. When someone develops an infection, the immune system recognizes the antigens and attempts to reject them. When somebody receives a donated organ, he or she is given immunosuppressant drugs to prevent organ rejection. The

THE FUNCTIONING OF GENES

Genes are units of chemical information that are found inside cells. They express themselves by directing the synthesis of proteins and are responsible for every trait that an organism shows. Genes are located on chromosomes, which are long strands of deoxyribonucleic acid (DNA) found in the nuclei of cells. Each gene is a unit of that DNA that codes for or dictates the production of a specific protein. That gene first makes a modified copy of itself called messenger RNA, which then travels from the nucleus into the cell's cytoplasm. There, a ribosome assembles the protein out of amino acids, as dictated by the sequence of specific subunits of the messenger RNA. Whenever DNA spontaneously changes, or mutates, the result is ultimately a change in the protein that is produced.

Proteins play a number of very important roles in the life of a cell. Some are responsible for how a cell, and therefore an organism, is put together. Others are chemical regulators, called enzymes, that control chemical reactions. In multicellular animals like ourselves, some proteins are produced in response to infection. Such proteins are known as antibodies. They function specifically in response to disease organisms or, in some cases, to chemical products of disease organisms, such as waste products.

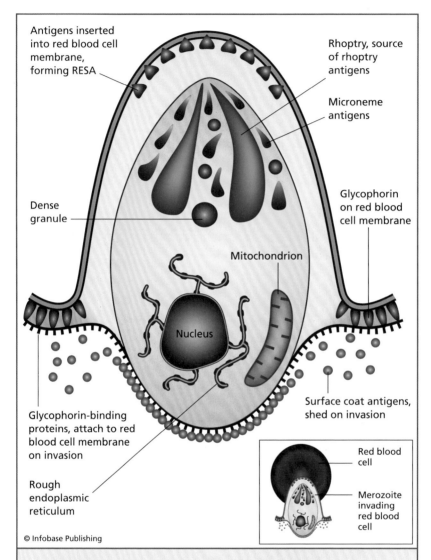

Figure 9.1 *Plasmodium* antigens are complex, as can be seen in this diagram. Antigens form on both the surface of the cell (such as antigens inserted into the cell membrane, top, and surface coat antigens). Other antigens form within the cell itself (microneme antigens). All types of antigens alert the immune system to the presence of a foreign object. The immune system then sends out antigens that attempt to destroy the invading cell.

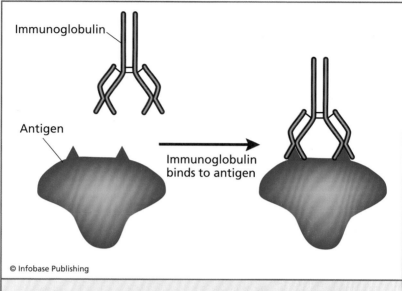

Immunoglobulin

Antigen

Immunoglobulin
binds to antigen

© Infobase Publishing

Figure 9.2 The human body creates antibodies in response to foreign antigens. These antibodies, shaped like a Y, attach to the foreign body at the antigen-presenting site and eventually destroy the invading organism before it can cause harm to the body.

organ recipient initially must be kept in an environment that is nearly sterile because of great risk of infection from suppression of the immune system.

In a healthy individual, the biochemical monitors that respond to antigens would typically respond to disease organisms. In nature, the response to a disease organism, the immune response, offers long-term, sometimes permanent, protection if it is successful. To bring about immune protection medically without inducing illness, doctors use **vaccines**.

In the case of malaria, the parasites involved in the initial attack are few in number. They circulate in the bloodstream for a very short time. Therefore, the immune system does not get much chance to detect them. Consequently, for a malarial vaccine to work, it would not only have to be administered before infection occurred, it would also have to be sufficiently modified to remain in circulation for enough time for the immune system to react.

Most successful vaccines have been developed to combat viral diseases, such as polio or smallpox. Some have been developed against bacterial diseases as well, but not as many. Viruses are genetically simple organisms. Bacteria, although more complex than viruses, are still relatively uncomplicated organisms.

Plasmodium, the protozoan that causes malaria is a eukaryote, an organism whose genetic material is concentrated in its cells' nuclei. Such organisms are genetically and biochemically more complex that the prokaryotic viruses and bacteria. Their complexity is exacerbated by sexual reproduction, which provides new genetic combinations with each generation. *Plasmodium* is able to change antigens quickly, which helps it hide from the immune system. Vaccines trick the immune system into producing antibodies in the absence of a true infection. Malaria, with its genetic complexity, produces thousands of antigens. Finding the right ones to put into a vaccine has been a challenge, because a vaccine that works against one set of malarial antigens will not work against altered ones.

To illustrate the problem of developing a vaccine for a genetically complex organism, influenza ("the flu") is genetically more complex than most viruses, changes antigens frequently, and keeps evolving resistance to vaccines. That is why new flu vaccines are needed every year. Because malaria is even more complex than the flu, developing an effective vaccine is much more difficult.

Certain political realities have stood in the way of developing a vaccine. Because malaria is most common in some of the poorest countries in the world, there has not been a lot of research money to support the search for new drugs or vaccines, nor are there abundant research facilities in which to do the work. Even Roll Back Malaria, an internationally funded program, can function only as long as the foundations and their sponsors are willing to continue providing funds. Malaria does not have the visibility of another plague that is also rampant in Africa with which it coexists and competes for research money: AIDS.

Unlike malaria, AIDS has a very real presence in the United States. AIDS is not the biggest killer in North America. Cardiovascular disease kills 50 times as many people. However, it reportedly garners much research money largely because it is

DISEASE PREVENTION BY VACCINATION

When a person develops an infectious disease, his or her body responds by producing proteins called antibodies, which protect the body. The antibodies are produced in response to antigens, usually proteins on the surface of the infecting organism. They may dissolve the antigens, they may cause them to clump together, or they may simply bind them up so that they can do no harm. This response is called an immune response. If the response is quick and strong enough, the person will recover from the infection. If not, he or she may die. When and if recovery occurs, the antibodies will remain protective, in some cases for life. This period of protection is immunity.

Immunity can be medically induced. If an antigen is medically introduced into a person, by a vaccine, the recipient will respond by developing antibodies, just as if he or she had the disease. A vaccine contains the antigens that will stimulate the production of antibodies.

Usually, the antigens that are introduced are not unadulterated disease germs. They have been weakened or killed. As long as intact antigens are present, however, our bodies cannot tell whether they are dangerous or not, and our immune system responds as if the antigen presents a real threat.

so visible. AIDS has affected celebrities. It has received attention from many celebrities and politicians. In contrast, malaria is well hidden. It does not have a cast of celebrities to advertise its existence. It does not occur, at the moment, in the United States. However, it continues to fester in Africa and Asia, and it continues to take lives daily. Continued support for malaria research is as important as is support for AIDS research.

Despite all of these obstacles, research on a malaria vaccine has continued and progress has been made. The Program for Appropriate Technology in Health (PATH) Malaria Vaccine Initiative has several candidate vaccines in development, and some are undergoing clinical trials as this is being written. Support for the work has been provided by the Bill and Melinda Gates Foundation, among others. It is hoped that one in particular, a vaccine that will trigger an immune response against *P. falciparum* sporozoites, the form injected by the mosquitoes, will be ready by 2010.

WHAT WILL THE FUTURE BRING WITH MALARIA?

Once again, the future is uncertain. There is no way of knowing, for example, if malaria will ever return to the United States in epidemic proportions. The reality is that it could.

It is highly probable that the research on malaria will lead to the successful development of a vaccine within the foreseeable future. However, this development will require ongoing research and support.

In addition to poverty and remoteness of the lands where it is now rampant, there are other obstacles to conquering malaria. In those places, population growth is very rapid, there is a lot of crowding, and sick people are sometimes lost within the masses. There is political instability in some of those places, and some are socially unstable as well. There is hunger as well as illness, and often there is no easy way of getting food and medicines to the people who need them. In order to be certain that the clinical trials for the malaria vaccine are evaluated correctly, it is essential that those vaccinated are accurately diagnosed as having developed the disease or not. Both false positive and false negative diagnoses could lead to inaccurate evaluations, resulting in both wasted time and wasted money. Diagnosis of malaria is still best done by microscopic examination of blood by skilled technicians. In Kismu, Kenya, a Malaria Diagnostics Centre of Excellence has been established to train technicians to do these diagnoses. Courses at the Diagnostics Centre that include exams and homework have resulted in improved skills of many of the technicians who participated. Participants have come from 11 countries in Africa.

Technically speaking, an effective vaccine against malaria is probable within the foreseeable future. But malaria is only one of many things that is competing for the attention of the limited scientific, medical, and humanitarian resources that are available, and getting the vaccine distributed could be problematic. One would hope that the problems with malaria, as well as all of the other problems facing the world today, will one day be solved. At this point, however, that remains to be seen.

Diseases such as mumps and rubella largely have been brought under control as a result of vaccination. Smallpox was eliminated from nature using vaccines. Some cultures of smallpox virus have been artificially maintained, some of them for the purpose of biological warfare. As described earlier, not all disease organisms lend themselves to vaccine production, however, vaccines seem to work best against viruses and, to a lesser extent, against bacteria. Parasitic protozoa and more complex parasites such as worms seem to be better able to hide from the immune system. Consequently, vaccines against them are much more challenging to produce. Consequently, the successful development of a malarial vaccine, once completed, will represent a monumental accomplishment.

Other promising strategies exist, and ongoing research continues to be conducted. One particularly exciting area is in the genetic modification of mosquitoes to render them

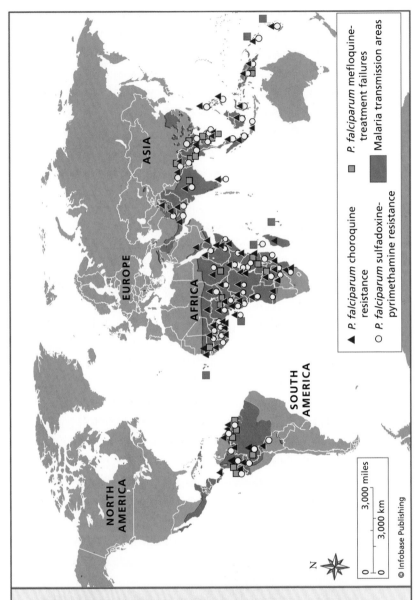

Figure 9.3 *Plasmodium falciparum* has become drug resistant in many areas of the world, as can be seen on this map. In some areas, *Plasmodium falciparum* is resistant to multiple drugs.

incapable of carrying malaria and other parasites. Specifically, male mosquitoes with engineered genes would be raised in laboratories and released to compete with wild-type males for females. Since female mosquitoes mate only once, each one that mates with a modified male would then pass on the modified genes to her offspring, thus, ideally, reducing the number of mosquitoes in subsequent generations that would be capable of housing or transmitting infectious parasites. It is an imaginative undertaking, but it could contribute toward a reduction of the deleterious impact malaria has on human health.

Malaria has been a dangerous companion of the human race for as long as the human race has existed and perhaps even longer. Fifty years ago, it seemed as if malaria would be eliminated. Today, malaria is once again rampant in much of the world, killing hundreds of thousands and making millions ill. Moreover, today numerous strains of malaria are resistant to many of the medications that have worked against them in the past. The mosquito vectors that spread the disease have developed resistance to many pesticides and drugs (Figure 9.3). Malaria stands ready to threaten much of the rest of the world as well. However, the integrated approach that is being taken in the battle against malaria gives one reason to hope that the disease may yet be conquered. Research into vaccines, medications, cultural changes, new safe and effective treatments, and even genetic modification of organisms may finally bring the disease under control.

Notes

Chapter 1

1. Louis Ortega, "Oral History: Battle of Guadalcanal, 1942–1943," Department of the Navy—Naval Historical Center, 2000, http://www.history.navy.mil/faqs/faq87-3c.htm (accessed August 22, 2008).
2. Centers for Disease Control and Prevention, "The Impact of Malaria, a Leading Cause of Death Worldwide," U.S. Department of Health and Human Services, http://www.cdc.gov/malaria/impact/index.htm (accessed August 19, 2008).

Chapter 2

1. V.S. Resh, "Mosquito Control and Habitat Modification: Case History Studies of San Francisco Bay Wetlands," *Bioasssessment and Management of North American Freshwater Wetlands* (Hoboken: Wiley and Sons, 2001), 413–428.
2. Centers for Disease Control and Prevention, "Malaria," U.S. Department of Health and Human Services, http://www.cdc.gov/malaria/disease.htm (accessed August 19, 2008).

Chapter 3

1. Robert S. Desowitz, *The Malaria Capers: Tales of Parasites and People* (New York: W.W. Norton & Company, 1993).
2. Margaret Humphreys, *Malaria: Poverty, Race, and Public Health in the United States* (Baltimore: Johns Hopkins University Press, 2001).
3. Giles Newton, "The Evolution of Malaria Parasites," Wellcome Trust, http://malaria.wellcome.ac.uk/doc_WTD023858.html (accessed August 19, 2008).
4. Ximena J. Nelson and Robert R. Jackson, "A Predator from East Africa That Chooses Malaria Vectors as Preferred Prey," *PLoS ONE*, 1: (2006), http://www.pubmedcentral.nih.gov/articlerender.fcgi?tool=pmcentrez&artid=1762417 (accessed August 19, 2008).
5. S. Wambua, et al., "The Effect of Alpha +-Thalassaemia on the Incidence of Malaria and Other Diseases in Children Living on the Coast of Kenya," *PLoS Medicine* 3, 5: (2006), http://www.pubmedcentral.nih.gov/articlerender.fcgi?artid=1435778 (accessed August 19, 2008).

Chapter 4

1. Ken W. Watson, "Malaria—a Rideau Mythconception," *Rideau Reflections* (Winter/Spring 2007), http://www.rideau-info.com/canal/articles/malaria.html (accessed August 22, 2008).

Chapter 5

1. Centers for Disease Control and Prevention. "Malaria: Diagnosis," U.S. Department of Heal and Human Services, http://www.cdc.gov/malaria/diagnosis_treatment/diagnosis.htm (accessed August 19, 2008).
2. M.L. Wilcox and G. Bodeker, "Traditional Herbal Medicines for Malaria," *BMJ* 329 (2004): 1156–1159, http://www.bmj.com/cgi/content/full/329/7475/1156 (accessed August 19, 2008).

Chapter 6

1. Centers for Disease Control and Prevention, "Eradication of Malaria in the United States, 1947–1951," U.S. Department of Health and Human Services, http://www.cdc.gov/malaria/history/eradication_us.htm (accessed August 19, 2008).
2. Department of Chemistry, Duke University, "Dangers of DDT," Department of Chemistry, Duke University, http://www.chem.duke.edu/~jds/cruise_chem/pest/effects.html#human (accessed August 19, 2008).
3. Qunhua Liv, et al. "New Irrigation Methods Sustain Malaria Control in Sichuan Province, China," *Acta Tropica*, 89, 2 (2004): 241–247.

Chapter 7

1. M.S. Fradin, "Mosquitoes and Mosquito Repellents: a Clinician's Guide," *Annals of Internal Medicine*, 128, 11 (1998): 931–940.

2. G.V.N.S. Kumar, R. Maheshwari, and K.H. Prabhu, "Recent Developments of Mosquito Repellent Textiles," *ATA—Journal for Asia on Textiles & Apparel* (December 2007), http://textile.2456.com/eng/epub/n_details.asp?epubiid=4&id=2182 (accessed March 2, 2008).

3. M.B. Nierengarten, "First Trial Results of a Blood-stage Malaria Vaccine Promising," *The Lancet Infectious Diseases*, 8, 3 (2008): 152.

4. R.M. Poole, "The Ethiopia Campaign," *Smithsonian*, 38, 3 (2007): 86–96, http://www.smithsonianmag.com/people-places/The_Ethiopia_Campaign.html (accessed August 19, 2008).

Chapter 8

1. "Malaria Surveillance—United States, 2000," *Morbidity and Mortality Weekly Report, CDC Surveillance Summaries : MMWR. CDC Surveillance Summaries*, 51 (2002): 9–11, http://www.cdc.gov/mmwr/preview/mmwrhtml/ss5105a2.htm (accessed August 19, 2008).

Glossary

alternative host—A host, other than a parasite's usual host, in which a parasite can survive and complete its life cycle.

alternation of generations—A life cycle characterized by alternating sexually and asexually reproducing generations.

antibiotic—A chemical usually produced by a microorganism that has the capacity to kill or otherwise inhibit other microorganisms but that is usually not sufficiently toxic to humans or other animals to prevent its use medically.

antibody—A blood protein that is produced in response to an infection and is toxic or otherwise inhibitory to the infecting organism.

antigen—A chemical, usually on the surface of a cell, that can stimulate the production of antibodies in an organism.

arthropod—An animal characterized by having a hard, jointed body covering, no internal skeleton, and paired, jointed legs.

bioaccumulation—The buildup of environmental toxins or contaminants in predatory animals or other higher-level consumers.

bioterrorism—Using biological agents such as disease germs or toxins in an act of war or in act of intimidating a population.

bioweapon—A biological agent, usually of a pathogenic nature, used to deliberately harm others.

DDT—Dichloro-diphenyl-trichloroethane, an insecticide used to kill mosquitoes.

definitive host—The host in which a parasite usually reaches sexual maturity.

diploid—The normal chromosome number in cells other than reproductive cells. It is characterized by chromosomes capable of being arranged in pairs, with one member of each pair donated by one of two parents. In humans, the diploid chromosome number is 46.

ecotourism—Tourism with the specific intent of visiting unique environments.

ectoparasite—An organism that lives on the surface of a host organism, obtains nourishment from the host, and can potentially cause harm.

endoparasite—An organism that lives within a host organism, obtains nourishment from the host, and can potentially cause harm.

haploid—The number of chromosomes normally found in a reproductive cell. It is equal to half of the diploid number, which in humans amounts to 23.

host—An organism on or in which a parasite lives.

immune response—The reaction of an organism to infection, often characterized by fever and the increased production of white blood cells.

immunity—Resistance to infection, often due to the presence of circulating antibodies in the bloodstream.

insecticide—A chemical used specifically to kill insects.

intermediate host—An organism in which a parasite must spend some of its life cycle but in which it does not reach sexual maturity.

lymphocyte—A white blood cell that participates in long-term immune responses, either by producing circulating antibodies or by producing cells that directly attack an antigen.

meiosis—The form of cell division in which haploid cells are produced. This usually occurs in the production of reproductive cells.

parasite—An organism that lives on or in a host organism, obtains its nourishment from the host, and has the potential of causing harm.

pathogen—An organism that specifically causes disease.

pesticide—A chemical that is used to kill or inhibit pest organisms.

protozoan—An organism composed of a single cell.

quinine—A compound isolated from the South American cinchona tree that was the first successful drug treatment for malaria.

reservoir host—The organism in which a parasite is normally found in nature.

vaccine—A chemical made from weakened or otherwise nonpathogenic antigens from infectious organisms that is medically administered to a person or animal in order to generate immunity.

vector—Usually, but not always, an ectoparasite that can transmit disease organisms among hosts.

zoonosis—A disease of animals that can be transmitted to and infect people.

Bibliography

Anderson, K.E. *Malaria, Mosquitoes and Mayhem.* Bethel, Conn.: Carlton Press, 1988.

Aslan, G., M. Ulukanligil, A. Seyrek, and O. Erel. "Diagnostic Performance Characteristics of Rapid Dipstick Test for *Plasmodium vivax* Malaria." *Membrias do Instituto Oswaldo Cruz On-line*, 95, no. 5, (2001): 683-686. Available at *http://memorias.loc.fiocruz.br/965/4147.pdf*

Attaran, A., R. Maharaj, and R. Lirof. "Ethical Debate: Doctoring Malaria Badly: The Global Campaign to Ban DDT." *British Medical Journal*, 321 (2000): 1403-1405.

Baldwin, C. *Sickle Cell Disease.* Chicago: Heinemann Library, 2003.

Ballard, C. *The Immune System.* Chicago: Heinemann Library, 2003.

Bannister, L.H., J.M. Hopkins, R.E. Fowler, S. Krishna, and G.H. Mitchell. "Encyclopedia of Malaria: Asexual Blood Stage." *Parasitology Today*, 16 (2000) 427-433.

Becker, N. *Mosquitoes and their Control.* New York: Kluwer Academic/Plenem, 2003.

Borza, N. "Some Observations on Malaria and the Ecology of Central Macedonia in Antiquity." *American Journal of Ancient History* 4, no. 1 (1979): 102-124.

Bwire, R. *Bugs in Armor: a Tale of Malaria and Soldiering.* Lincoln, Nebr.: IUniverse, 2000.

Carson, R.L. *Silent Spring.* New York: Houghton Mifflin, 1962.

Cartwright, F.F. and M. Biddis. *Disease and History* 2nd ed., Phoenix Mill, U.K.: Sutton, 2000.

Casman, E.A., and H. Dowlatabadi, eds. *The Contextual Determinants of Malaria.* Washington, D.C.: Resources for the Future, 2002.

Chernin, J. *Parasitology.* New York: Taylor and Francis, 2000.

Clements, A.N. *The Biology of Mosquitoes: Vol. 2: Sensory Reception and Behaviour.* New York: Oxford University Press. 1999.

Crepley, I.M., D.N.J. Lockwood, D. Mack, G. Pasvol, and R.N. Davidson. "Rapid Diagnosis of *Falciparum* Malaria by using ParaSight F Test in Travellers Returning to the United Kingdom: Prospective Study." *British Medical Journal*, 321 (2002): 484-485.

Commoner, B. *The Closing Circle.* New York: Bantam Books, 1972.

Day, N. *Malaria, West Nile, and other Mosquito-Borne Diseases*. Berkely Heights, N.J.: Enslow, 2001.

Davis, K. *Cracking the Genome: Inside the Race to Unlock Human DNA*. Baltimore: Johns Hopkins University Press, 2002.

Desalle, R. *Epidemic! The World of Infectious Disease*. New York: The New Press, 1999.

Diamond, J. *Guns, Germs, and Steel: the Fates of Human Societies*. New York: W.W. Norton, 1997.

Donaldson, R.J., ed. *Parasites and Western Man*. Baltimore: University Park Press, 1979.

Doolan, D.L., ed. *Malaria: Methods and Protocols*. Totowa, N.J.: Humana Press, 2003.

DuTemple, L.A. *The Panama Canal*. Minneapolis: Lerner, 2002.

Ewald, P.W. *Evolution of Infectious Disease*. New York: Oxford University Press, 1994.

Fradin, M.S. "Mosquitoes and Mosquito Repellents: A Clinician's Guide." *Annals of Internal Medicine*, 128 (June, 1998): 931-940.

Freudenrich, C.C. "How Mosquitoes Work." *How Stuff Works*, 2000. Available online. URL: *http://www.howstuffworks.com*.

Harrison, G. *Malaria, Mosquitoes, and Man: A History of Hostilities Since 1880*. New York: Dutton, 1978.

Hausmann, K., and N. Hülsmann. *Protozoology*. New York: Thieme Medical Publishers, 1996.

Honigsbaum, M. *The Fever Trail: In Search of the Cure for Malaria*. New York: Picador, 2003.

Jarcho, S. *Quinine's Predecessor: Francisco Torti and the Early History of Cinchona*. Baltimore: John's Hopkins University Press, 1993.

Karlen, A. *Men and Microbes: Disease and Plagues in History and Modern Times*. New York: Simon & Schuster, 1996.

"Malaria, Mosquitoes, and DDT." *World Watch*, 15, no. 3 (May/June 2002).

Matteson, P. *Resolving the DDT Dilemma: Protecting Biodiversity and Human Health*. Collingdale, Pa.: Diane Publishing, 2002.

McNeill, W.H. *Plagues and People*. Harden City, N.Y.: Anchor Press, 1976.

Mohr, N. *Malaria: Evolution of a Killer.* Seattle, Wash.: Serif & Pixel Press, 2001.

Morrison, P., and P. Morrison. "Roll Back Malaria." *Scientific American* (January, 2000).

Oldstone, M.B. *Viruses, Plagues, and History.* New York: Oxford University Press, 2000.

Pampana, E. *Textbook of Malaria Eradication.* New York: Oxford University Press, 1970.

Poser, C.M., and G.W. Bruyn. *An Illustrated History of Malaria.* New York: Parthenon, 1999.

Reid, A.J.C., C.S.M. Whitty, H.M. Ayles, R.M. Jennings, B.A. Bovill, J.M. Felton, R.H. Behrens, A.D.M. Bryceson, and D.C.W. Mabey. "Malaria at Christmas: Risks of Prophylaxis versus Risks of Malaria." *British Medical Journal,* 317 (1998): 1506-1508.

Schmidt, G.D., L.S. Roberts, and J. Janovy Jr. *Foundations of Parasitology.* New York: McGraw-Hill Science/Engineering/Math, 1995.

Scientific American. "A Death Every 30 Seconds." June, 2002. Available online. URL: *http://www.sciam.com.*

"Scientist Discovers Mosquito Repellent in Tomatoes." *Science News,* June 11, 2002. Available online. URL: *http://www.cosmiverse.com/news/science/science06110103.html*

Sellares, R. *Malaria and Rome: A History of Malaria in Ancient Italy.* New York: Oxford University Press, 2002.

Shulka, O.P. *Pesticides, Man and Biosphere.* New Delhi, India: Ashish, 1998.

Spielman, A., and M. D'Antonio. *Mosquito: A Natural History of our most Persistent and Deadly Foe.* New York: Hyperion, 2001.

Sugden, A.L. and J. Chamberlain, eds. *Malaria: Current Topics & Reviews.* Champaign, Ill.: Pharmaceutical Press, 1997.

Sutherland, D.J., and W.J. Crans. *Mosquitoes in Your Life.* New Jersey Agriculture Experiment Station Publication SA220-5M-86, 1986. Available online. URL: *http://www-rci.Rutgers.edu/~insects/moslife.htm.*

Sweeny, A.W. "Prospects for Control of Mosquito-Borne Diseases." *Journal of Medical Microbiology,* 48, no. 10 (1999): 879-881.

Textbook of Malaria Eradication. New York: Oxford University Press, 1970.

Travis, J. "Blood Cues Sex Choices for Parasite." *Science News Online,* January 8, 2000. Available online. URL: *http://www.findarticles.com/cf_dis/m1200/2_157/58726365/p1/article.*

Tren, R., R. Bate, and H.M. Koenig. *Malaria and the DDT Story.* London: Institute of Economic Affairs, 2001.

Turkington, C.A. *Ills and Conditions: Malaria.* 1999. Available online. URL: *http://www.principalhealthnews.com/topic/malaria.*

Walker, H. "We Remember . . . The Erie Canal," Newark, N.Y.: *The Newark Courier Gazette,* March 18, 1998. Available online: URL: *http://cgazette.com/towns/Newark/history/918323473038.htm.*

Warrell, D.A., and H.M. Gilles. *Essential Malariology,* 4th ed. London: Edward Arnold, 2002.

Watts, S. *Epidemics and History: Disease, Power, and Imperialism.* New Haven, Conn.: Yale University Press, 1997.

Williams, G. *The Plague Killers.* New York: Charles Scribner's. 1969.

Wong, K. Combating Malaria. *Scientific American.* October, 2000. Available online. URL: *http://www.sciam.com.*

———. "Research Challenges Proposed Link Between Malaria Growth and Global Warming." *Scientific American.* February, 2002. Available at *http://www.sciam.com*

World Health Organization. *DDT and its Derivatives: Environmental Aspects.* Albany, N.Y.: World Health Organization, 1989.

———. *Vector Control for Malaria and other Mosquito-Borne Diseases: Report of a WHO Study Group.* Albany, N.Y.: World Health Organization, 1995.

World Watch Institute. *State of the World: 2003.* New York: W.W. Norton, 2002.

Zookerman, J.N. *Essentials of Travel Medicine.* Hoboken, N.J.: John Wiley, 2003.

Further Resources

Books and Articles

Causer, L.M. 2002. "Malaria surveillance —United States, 2000," *C.D.C. Morbidity & Mortality Weekly Report* July 12, 2002, 51 (SS05): 9-21. Available online. URL: http://www.cdc.gov/mmwr/preview/mmwrhtml/ss5105a2. htm. Accessed March 4, 2008.

Centers for Disease Control and Prevention. "Eradication of Malaria in the United States (1947-1951," U.S. Department of Health and Human Services. Available online. URL: http://www.cdc.gov/malaria/history/eradication_ us.htm. Accessed February 29, 2008.

Centers for Disease Control and Prevention. "The impact of Malaria, a Leading Cause of Death Worldwide," U.S. Department of Heal and Human Services. Available online. URL: http://www.cdc.gov/malaria/impact/index. htm. Accessed February 24, 2008.

Centers for Disease Control and Prevention. "Malaria," U.S. Department of Heal and Human Services. Available online. URL: http://www.cdc.gov/ malaria/disease.htm. Accessed March 19, 2008.

Centers for Disease Control and Prevention. "Malaria: Diagnosis," U.S. Department of Health and Human Services. Available online. URL: http:// www.cdc.gov/malaria/diagnosis_treatment/diagnosis.htm. Accessed February 29, 2008.

D'Alessandro, U. 2001. "Insecticide treated bed nets to prevent Malaria." *BMJ* Vol. 322 No. 7281 Pp. 249-250. Available online. URL: http://www.pubmedcentral. nih.gov/articlerender.fcgi?artid=1119510. Accessed April 6, 2008

Department of Chemistry, Duke University. "Dangers of DDT," Department of Chemistry, Duke University. Available online. URL: http://www.chem.duke. edu/~jds/cruise_chem/pest/effects.html#human. Accessed March 1, 2008.

Desowitz, R.S. 1991. *The Malaria Capers: Tales of Parasites and People.* New York, W.W. Norton & Company.

Fradin, M.S. 1998. "Mosquitoes and mosquito repellents: a clinician's guide," *Annals of Internal Medicine* Vol. 128 No. 11, Pp 931-940.

Gould, F., K. Magori, and Y. Huang. 2006. Genetic strategies for controlling mosquito-borne diseases. *American Scientist* Vol. 94 No. 3. Pp. 238-246.

"Hopes of Malaria Vaccine by 2010," *BBC News.* Available online. URL: http:// news.bbc.co.uk/2/hi/health/3742876.stm. Accessed April 30, 2008.

Humphreys, M. 2001. *Malaria: Poverty, Race, and Public Health in the United States.* Baltimore, MD, The Johns Hopkins University Press.

Ipca Laboratories Ltd. "*Crusade against Malaria.* Available online. URL: http://www.malaria-ipca.com/index.htm. Accessed March 3, 2008.

Kumar, G.V.N.S., R. Maheshwari, and K.H. Prabhu. 2007. "Recent Developments of Mosquito Repellent Textiles," *ATA—Journal for Asia on Textiles & Apparel* December. Available online. URL: http://textile.2456.com/eng/epub/n_details.asp?epubiid=4&id=2182. Accessed March 2, 2008.

Liu, Qunhua, K Xin, C. Changzhi, F. Shengzheng, L. Yan, H. Rongzhi, Z. Zhihua, G. Gibson, and K. Wenmin. 2004. "New irrigation methods sustain malaria control in Sichuan Province, China. *Acta Tropica* Vol. 89 No. 2. Pp 241-247.

Nchinda, T.C. 1998. "Malaria: A Reemerging Disease in Africa." *Emerging Infectious Diseases* Vol. 4, No. 3. Available online. URL: http://www.cdc.gov/ncidod/eid/vol4no3/nchinda.htm. Accessed April 3, 2008.

Nelson, X.J. and R.R. Jackson. 2006 "A Predator from East Africa that Chooses Malaria Vectors as Preferred Prey," *PLoS ONE,* 1(1). Available online. URL: http://www.pubmedcentral.nih.gov/articlerender.fcgi?tool=pmcentrez&artid=1762417. Accessed February 21, 2004.

Newton, G. "The Evolution of Malaria Parasites," Wellcome Trust. Available online. URL: http://malaria.wellcome.ac.uk/doc_WTD023858.html. Accessed February 27, 2008.

Nierengarten, M.B. 2008. 2008. "First Trial Results of a Blood-stage Malaria Vaccine Promising." *The Lancet Infectious Diseases* Vol. 8 No.3. P. 152.

Poole, R.M. 2007. "The Ethiopia Campaign," *Smithsonian* Vol. 38 No. 3. Pp. 86-96.

Wambua, S. et al. 2006. "The Effect of α^+-thalassaemia on the Incidence of Malaria and Other Diseases in Children Living on the Coast of Kenya," *PLoS Med* 3(5). Available online. URL: http://www.pubmedcentral.nih.gov/articlerender.fcgi?artid=1435778. Accessed March 13, 2008.

Wilcox, M.L. and G. Bodeker. 2004. "Traditional Herbal Medicines for Malaria," *BMJ* 329:1156-1159. Available online. URL: http://www.bmj.com/cgi/content/full/329/7475/1156. Accessed March 16, 2008.

Web Sites

The American Mosquito Control Association
http://www.mosquito.org

Further Resources

The Carter Center Malaria Control Program
http://www.cartercenter.org/health/malaria_control/unique.html

Bill and Melinda Gates Foundation Global Health
http://www.gatesfoundation.org/GlobalHealth/pri-Diseases/Malaria/default.htm

Global Fund to Fight AIDS, Tuberculosis, and Malaria
http://www.theglobalfund.org/EN/

Malaria Foundation International
http://www.malaria.org

Malaria No More
http://www.malarianomore.org

Malaria Site
http://www.malariasite.com

National Library of Medicine
http://www.nlm.nih.gov

Roll Back Malaria Partnership
http://www.rbm.who.int

Sickle Cell Disease Association of America
http://sicklecelldisease.org

U.S. Environmental Protection Agency
http://www.epa.gov

The Wellcome Trust
http://wellcome.ac.uk

World Health Organization
http://www.who.int

Index

About the Author

Bernard A. Marcus, Ph.D. is professor emeritus of biology at Genesee Community College in Batavia, New York. His principal interests have been in environmental biology, particularly aquatics, and the modeling of aquatic environments in the laboratory. He has been involved in studies on New York's Finger Lakes, the impact of acid precipitation in the Adirondack Mountains, and the effects of water pollution on stream insects. More recently he has become interested in tropical biology and has been leading student trips to the rainforests of Central America. His recreational activities include fishing, hiking, and model railroading.

About the Consulting Editor

Hilary Babcock, M.D., M.P.H., is an Assistant Professor of Medicine at Washington University School of Medicine and the Medical Director of Occupational Health for Barnes-Jewish Hospital and St. Louis Children's Hospital. She received her undergraduate degree from Brown University and her M.D. from the University of Texas Southwestern Medical Center at Dallas. After completing her residency, chief residency, and infectious disease fellowship at Barnes-Jewish Hospital, she joined the faculty of the Infectious Disease division. She completed an M.P.H. in Public Health from St. Louis University School of Public Health in 2006. She has lectured, taught, and written extensively about infectious diseases, their treatment, and their prevention. She is a member of numerous medical associations and is board certified in infectious disease. She lives in St. Louis, Missouri.